Measuring the value of knowledge management

By Joanna Goodman

Contents

ACKNOWLEDGEMENTS	iii
EXECUTIVE SUMMARY	1

PART 1

CHAPTER 1
The ROI of KM: determining the relevant metrics — 3
- Key challenges — 3
- The value wheel — 4
- Using KPIs to uncover the ROI on KM activities — 5
- A macro approach: linking KM with overall business strategy — 6
- A micro approach: determining the return on specific KM activities — 6
- The human factor: sharing knowledge and replicating best practice — 6
- Making it personal: the WIFM factor — 6
- The time factor — 7

CHAPTER 2
The business case for measurement — 9
- KM's business drivers — 9
- The strategic role of KM measurement — 9
- Compelling reasons to measure — 10

CHAPTER 3
Measurement methodologies — 13
- KM as a business expense — 13
- Clare and Detore's six-step KM valuation model — 13
- Performance measures — 14
- The Balanced Scorecard — 15
- Assessing the benefits of KM — 16
- Skyrme Associates' benefit tree — 16
- Evaluating intangible assets and intellectual capacity — 17
- Measuring specific initiatives — 19
- KM maturity models — 20

CHAPTER 4
How to measure: tools and tactics that work — 23
- Link measures to strategy — 23
- Six steps to effective KM measurement — 23

Set clear parameters	24
Choose appropriate measures	24
Start small: pilot projects demonstrate ROI and value	26
Know your audience: communicate meaningful metrics	26
A practical demonstration of value	27

PART 2

CHAPTER 5
The Superknowledge Declaration — 29

CHAPTER 6
The value of knowledge doesn't exist — 33

A framework for valuing the potential of knowledge	33
A framework for valuing knowledge	34
A mathematical formulation for knowledge-based value creation	34
Knowledge relevance indicator	36
Knowledge connectivity factor	37
Knowledge activation factor	37
Added value in context	38
Knowledge capturing and learning	38
Summary conclusion and next steps	38

CHAPTER 7
E-learning and know-how within BAE Systems — 41

CHAPTER 8
A value judgement:
Demonstrating the worth of knowledge management – Berwin Leighton Paisner — 45

Differing approaches to measurement	45
Some challenges	45
Initial considerations	46
Three suggested methodologies	46
List of KPIs	47
ARC model	47
Balanced Scorecard	48
Demonstrating value	48

CHAPTER 9
Collaboration and beyond – Caterpillar — 51

History and evolution of the KN	51
Value chain collaboration	51
Growth rates	52

The KN in action	52
Community roles	53
Security issues	53
Types of communications	54
Reference material on the KN	54
Value to the organisation	54

CHAPTER 10
Measuring and demonstrating the value of KM – Fluor Corporation — 57

Why KM at Fluor?	57
The benefits of KM at Fluor	58
Where we are now	58
Creating value	59

CHAPTER 11
Applying KM to improve quality – Ford — 63

Quality improvement is taken seriously	65
What are the results of these efforts?	65
Why use KM to leverage quality efforts?	65
Getting maximum value of quality-improvement efforts	65
What have we learnt about how to apply KM to improve quality?	66

CHAPTER 12
Halliburton: A sustained commitment to collaboration — 69

The history	69
The approach	70
The value proposition	70
Case history: SAP procurement and material	71
Case history: Electronic Technician Community	72
Relationship to hierarchy	73

CHAPTER 13
Answering the question – Lucent Technologies — 77

Ask Lucent	77
Business objectives	78
Deployment framework	78
The next phase	80
The final phase	82
ROI and other benefits	83

CHAPTER 14
A competency-based framework for knowledge and learning – Overseas Development Institute — 85

The RAPID programme	86

ODI's strategic approach	87
Strategy development	87
The Five Competencies Framework	89

CHAPTER 15
A debate on monitoring and evaluating KM activities – KM4Dev — 93

The first level of discussions	93
The second level of discussions	93
The third level of discussions	94

CHAPTER 16
Ricardo: Driven by knowledge — 95

Sources of input knowledge	95
Taming input knowledge	96
Achieving competitive knowledge	96
Knowledge products and services	97

CHAPTER 17
Identifying Ricardo's knowledge assets — 101

Distinguishing knowledge from other assets	101
Intangible	101
Archives	102
Patents	102
Assimilated knowledge	102
The Ricardo knowledgebase	104
Tacit knowledge	104
Explicit knowledge	105
Embedded knowledge	105
Conclusion	105

CHAPTER 18
KM Scorecards at Unisys — 107

Knowledge management vision	107
The KM Scorecard	107
Project Scorecards	108
Example project: Engagement Knowledgebase	108
KM outcomes	111

INDEX — 115

Acknowledgements

SPECIAL THANKS to all those who have given up their time to research and write a case study for inclusion in this report: Victo Newman; Paul Iske; Thijs Boekhoff; Richard West; Lucy Dillon; Reed Stuedemann; Rob E.V. Koene; Sanjay Swarup; Jerry Ash; Simon Walker; Ben Ramalingam; Martin Ward; and Alex Goodall. Finally, thanks to all those, too numerous to list here, who have shared their accumulated knowledge and understanding, through *Inside Knowledge* magazine and Ark Group's series of knowledge-management related events.

Executive Summary

IN TODAY'S highly competitive, technology-driven business environment, few enterprises have the luxury of allocating resources to internal programmes and initiatives such as KM without being required to demonstrate their value. So what return on investment (ROI) can organisations expect to achieve from investing money and resources in KM? What is the best way to determine the relevant metrics?

This report aims to provide managers and practitioners with knowledge management (KM) and internal communications responsibilities with some answers. It encapsulates a selection of the most popular measurement methodologies developed by well-known KM experts, including Melissie Clemmons Rumizen, Wesley Vestal, Karl-Erik Sveiby and Leif Edvinsson, the world's first professor of intellectual capital, to name but a few, with up-to-date tools and tactics for establishing ROI on KM resources, initiatives and activities.

Part 1 covers the what, why and how of KM measurement, drawing on the latest thinking from experts in the field, including thought-provoking guidance from KM practitioners at leading organisations who have contributed case studies to Ark Group's *Ei* and *Inside Knowledge* magazines over the past 18 months.

Chapter 1 looks at the challenge of measuring the value of KM and quantifying the tangible and intangible returns, using Jim Bair's value wheel to illustrate how the interdependence of KM activities – incorporating processes, technology and people – and outcomes produces direct and indirect returns that can be used to demonstrate a clear ROI on KM. It goes on to describe how linking KM activities and initiatives to overall corporate strategy channels KM to support the delivery of key business objectives throughout the business and drive competitive advantage. It shows how linking KM to your organisation's key performance indicators helps to uncover the substantial hard and soft benefits that make up the ROI of effective KM. Hard or quantifiable returns include:

- Labour savings;
- Reinvestment of resources;
- Cost reduction; and
- Cost avoidance.

Examples of soft (or indirect) returns include:

- Knowledge re-use;
- Leveraged knowledge resources;
- Reduced time to market; and
- Customer satisfaction.

Parallel to this macro approach is a micro approach, whereby applying measurement processes to specific KM activities helps to differentiate its contribution and uncover the key metrics for determining its ROI.

Chapter 2 defines the business case and explores some of the compelling business reasons to measure the value of your KM programme. Establishing a clear ROI on KM provides meaningful metrics to justify the ongoing costs of knowledge resources and initiatives to senior managers and other stakeholders, who are looking for hard dollar returns, thereby gaining leadership buy-in and support for KM activities and ensuring the continued allocation of resources. It goes on to demonstrate how ongoing measurement supports effective KM by showing the extent to which KM strategies are being implemented,

Executive summary
Measuring the Value of Knowledge Management

providing feedback, identifying scope for improvement and communicating KM strategy throughout the business. Finally, it outlines how meaningful metrics can be used to drive innovation and protect valuable intellectual capital by encouraging KM behaviours that deliver substantial and sustainable results.

Although KM is notoriously difficult to quantify, there is general agreement that KM measurement requires a mixture of quantitative and qualitative measures based on lagging and leading indicators. The best combination for any organisation will depend on its business profile, its key performance indicators and critical success factors, and its approach to KM. Chapter 3 reviews some of the most popular methodologies for measuring the impact of KM activities and initiatives on business results. First, we explore ways of differentiating and measuring the specific costs and benefits of KM and establishing its unique positive contribution to the balance sheet. These include Martin's cost of information formula, performance measures such as Kaplan and Norton's balanced scorecard, Clare and Detore's six-step valuation model and Skyrme Associates' benefits tree. As intangible assets represent an increasing proportion of a company's market capital, we explore a selection of intellectual capital measurement approaches for calculating the projected return on innovation investment – a critical success factor in many leading industries. Having outlined the straightforward approach documented by the US Department of the Navy, which categorises KM measures into systems, output and outcomes, the chapter concludes with the American Productivity and Quality Center (APQC) KM maturity model, which highlights the need to align KM measurement to the maturity of its KM programme.

Chapter 4 moves from theory to practice, outlining some of the best practices recommended by business gurus and KM experts. These include KM tools such as:

- Six steps to effective KM measurement;
- Knowledge mapping and auditing; and
- Pilot projects and after action reviews.

It then outlines practical tactics that have supported leading KM organisations in developing measurement strategies and processes which enable them to maximise the ROI on their KM activities and help them maintain their position as industry leaders in these competitive times. These include identifying the appropriate metrics, communicating them to different stakeholders, uncovering the stories behind the statistics and encouraging KM behaviours by highlighting the benefits to individual employees.

Part 2 comprises a selection of best-practice examples of KM measurement in action with practical, up-to-date case studies from leading organisations that have successfully developed KM measurement programmes to demonstrate the outstanding benefits that they have achieved by investing in KM initiatives and activities, including communities of practice, best practice replication, expertise locators and self-service online learning. Some of these were written for Ark Group's *Ei* and *Inside Knowledge* magazines, while others were produced specifically for this report. Participating organisations include Fluor Corporation, a 2006 Global MAKE (Most Admired Knowledge Enterprise) winner, Ford Motor Company, BAE Systems, Berwin Leighton Paisner, Caterpillar Inc, Halliburton, Lucent Technologies, the Overseas Development Institute and Ricardo; guidance from internationally recognised KM experts, including Jerry Ash, Victor Newman and Paul Louis Iske, is also examined.

1. The ROI of KM: Determining the relevant metrics

THE RETURN on investment (ROI) of knowledge management (KM) relates to the contribution to the success of an enterprise of investing time, money and resources in KM processes and activities – the capture, transfer and flow of information, expertise and best practice within a company. KM can be defined as the way in which an organisation leverages its collective tangible and intangible knowledge assets to add value to the business; therefore its ROI is a key indicator of the success of any KM programme. Effective KM contributes to business success by encouraging and exploiting knowledge flow to support an organisation's mission and vision and enabling it to deliver its strategic objectives more efficiently and effectively. However, the associated costs are significant and executives and other stakeholders are entitled to ask what specific benefits they might expect to gain from KM activities. This report makes the business case for measuring and evaluating KM with a view to determining its ROI – or its contribution to corporate performance and competitive advantage.

The direct positive correlation between effective KM and outstanding business performance is increasingly acknowledged – and documented in hundreds of case studies, including those in part 2 of this report. The findings of the 2006 Most Admired Knowledge Enterprise (MAKE) study, conducted by Teleos, in which a panel of global Fortune 500 senior executives and internationally recognised knowledge management/intellectual capital experts select 20 organisations that they consider to be global knowledge leaders, demonstrate that successfully managing enterprise knowledge yields big dividends. The 2006 global MAKE winners trading on the NYSE/NASDAQ showed a total return to shareholders for the ten-year period 1995-2005 of 24.2 percent – more than twice the average Fortune 500 company median.[1]

According to Rory Chase, managing director of Teleos, the fact that these companies are consciously building their knowledge portfolios enables them to outperform their competitors. It follows, therefore, that successful organisations need to be able to measure the value and the contribution of their KM initiatives and resources in order to develop and build on these critical success factors further. However, this is more easily said – or written – than done.

Key challenges

Determining the contribution of KM to an enterprise's overall success raises several key challenges. As Jim Bair[2] argues in Making Knowledge Work, "Returns on KM investments are not achieved through simplistic formulas. Successful KM depends on many variables." This is because KM involves combining tangible – and therefore quantifiable – resources and processes with the intangibles that underpin knowledge flow, such as working and customer relationships, workplace culture and management skill, which are notoriously difficult to measure.

The inherent difficulty in determining a clear return on the hybrid discipline of KM is exacerbated by the fact that the traditional balance sheet doesn't take account of key intangibles such as knowledge sharing, collaboration and innovation. As Lucy Dillon at Berwin Leighton Paisner (see chapter 8) explains, it is also difficult to distinguish performance improvements as having been derived solely from KM activities. Bair suggests that the impact of KM is difficult to quantify without a thorough understanding of the complete system. His value wheel is a graphic illustration of the ROI on KM being derived from a continuous process, "showing different outcomes running together in a cycle of hard, direct returns and soft, indirect returns."[3]

The value wheel

This model, illustrated in Figure 1, demonstrates how the interdependence of outcomes producing direct and indirect returns can demonstrate a clear ROI on KM. It incorporates processes, people and technology, all of which are central to achieving an ROI on KM. Bair emphasises that continuity and interdependence are crucial to achieving value. "The most important example is the relationship between labour savings and reinvestment, which is critical to gaining any ROI at all," he argues. "Saved labour must be reinvested in a valuable activity or potential gains will simply be lost in longer coffee breaks."

As Bair explains, the value wheel shows different outcomes running together in a cycle of hard, direct returns and soft, indirect returns that together contribute to strategic competitive advantage. Direct or hard, quantifiable returns include:

- Labour savings – for example, re-using elements of an existing report rather than writing one from scratch, or replicating a more efficient business process produces quantifiable savings.
- Reinvestment of resources – for example, if an activity is completed more efficiently, whatever savings are made may be redirected to complete more work in the same time.
- Cost reduction – if KM means that an activity requires fewer people and takes less time, the savings are obvious.
- Cost avoidance – improved efficiency increases capacity and productivity, thereby avoiding unnecessary costs.

Bair argues that because activities producing labour savings and reinvestment of resources are discretionary, they require the buy-in of an organisation's employee population. People need to be motivated by personal ROI, such as the chance to earn a pay rise, promotion, recognition, personal development or simply to save time and effort in their day-to-day roles and functions. Indirect or soft returns on KM include:

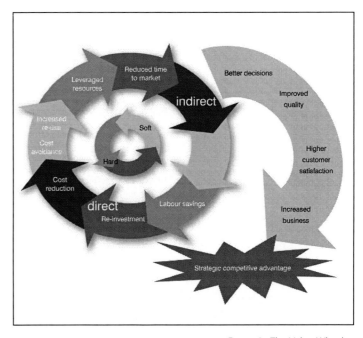

Figure 1: The Value Wheel
Source: Bair, J., Making Knowledge Work, Ark Group 2005

- Increased re-use – Bair describes this as the "management" in KM: capturing knowledge and re-using it. Knowledge is almost always applied in decision-making and KM adds what is necessary to take knowledge from one situation and apply it in others.
- Leveraged resources – this relates to enabling ubiquitous access to an organisation's collective expertise, information and data. Bair explains that this is not just about access; it's also about ensuring that everyone knows precisely what resources are available and underlines the importance of integrated enterprise-wide search capabilities. In this way KM infuses technology into day-to-day working practices.
- Reduced time to market – making knowledge available more quickly and cheaply reduces the time required for any project, increasing the potential ROI.
- Improved decision-making and a better balance between short and long-term objectives – this relates to the contribution of KM activities that enable collaboration and result in better-informed decision-making. As Bair puts it, "All that has to happen for KM to achieve a positive ROI is for a merger/acquisition to work, a pricing strategy to attract new customers or a new investment to yield increased productivity."
- Improved quality – relates to applying knowledge to improve business processes or customer relationships.
- Better response times – lead to higher customer satisfaction and loyalty.
- Increased business – result from quality and customer satisfaction improvements.
- Competitive advantage – this is derived from KM-enabled improved quality, customer satisfaction and increased business as outlined above.

Although these indirect benefits have significant positive financial impact, it is notoriously difficult to establish their precise contribution. The most effective measurement methodologies involve a combination of hard and soft metrics. Several of these are explored further in chapters 3 and 4 of this report.

Using KPIs to uncover the ROI on KM activities

Experts agree that the first step towards determining meaningful metrics for measuring KM activities in any organisation is to identify their key performance indicators (KPIs). Although these will necessarily vary from organisation to organisation according to the business profile of the enterprise, its core strategic objectives and its internal and external business environment, they can be organised into three categories, combining macro and micro approaches to build a rich picture of where KM adds value to the organisation:

- Business-based KPIs, which can be identified by linking KM with the organisation's overall strategic objectives;
- Process-based KPIs, which can be identified by analysing specific projects and KM and other initiatives; and
- Time-based KPIs, which relate to labour savings, best practice replication and faster response times.

A methodology based on KPIs takes into account many of the intangible, but highly significant, factors that contribute to the return on KM activities such as collaboration, innovation and developing a knowledge-sharing culture, as well as KM activities that are more easily monitored, such as providing access to information and expertise via online resources, communities and networks.

A macro approach: linking KM with overall business strategy

Business-based KPIs help to identify how KM supports the organisation in delivering its overall strategy. These are highlighted by linking KM activities such as sharing and re-using information and knowledge resources with specific enterprise-wide outcomes that contribute to enhanced business performance and competitive advantage, such as more efficient processes, higher productivity, reduced labour costs and increased innovation.

A micro approach: determining the return on specific KM activities

Analysing specific KM activities helps to determine the cost involved in creating, implementing and maintaining knowledge resources, including online information, people directories and training people to use them, facilitating networks and communities of practice (CoPs) and employing KM staff. These costs can then be set against the benefits of less time being spent searching for information, such as increased efficiency, faster response times and new business wins. Tracking the usage of particular online resources provides hard metrics that can be used to calculate their value.

For example, the ROI of stand-alone KM initiatives such as CoPs can be determined relatively accurately by various means, including tracking the level and type of participation. Meaningful metrics can be developed by forming control groups and comparing the performance of CoP members with that of non-members, and by comparing business results before and after the establishment of a particular CoP according to specific corporate objectives.

Assessing the impact of KM on different business units also provides an indication of how inclusive KM activities are, and where and how they contribute to the success of the enterprise.

The human factor: sharing knowledge and replicating best practice

Looking at KM in terms of process-based KPIs highlights the benefits resulting from leveraging knowledge and skills to improve processes and replicate best practice across the enterprise. Changing processes, particularly enterprise-wide, can be costly, so the investment of time and money, for example in business re-engineering or training people to work differently, needs to be set against the benefits that accrue to the organisation. Hard benefits, including efficiency and productivity improvements, can be supported by soft tactics, such as storytelling, as anecdotal evidence motivates people to replicate best practice. Of course, the benefits of storytelling can be quantified. If people hear that X group introduced Y measure and saved the company Z pounds, they are more likely to follow suit.

Soft returns that have a significant impact on business results include developing an organisational culture where people are willing to share their knowledge and expertise, and are flexible enough to change the way they work.

Making it personal: the WIFM factor

In *KM in the Legal Profession*, Bob Bater[4] refers to the significance of the 'What's in it for Me?' (WIFM) factor – the contribution of individual ROI in respect of maximising the return on KM achieved for the organisation. Incentives for knowledge sharing include career opportunities and an enhanced workplace experience. Less obvious motivators include recognition, the chance to work on challenging assignments and opportunities for personal development. Self-service online learning opportunities such as those at BAE Systems (see chapter 7) benefit individuals and the organisation as they give individuals control over their professional development and reduce training costs. At Fluor (see chapter 10), people are a key factor so it's important to keep them motivated by consistently communicating the value of knowledge sharing.

The time factor

Time is highly significant in determining the return on KM. Of course, saving time contributes directly to competitive advantage, as improved response times tend to have a positive effect on customer satisfaction and are therefore key to winning and retaining business. In an article for Inside Knowledge, Sarah Adams[5] of global insurer Aon describes how communities of practice help to give local offices faster access to enterprise-wide knowledge and information, leading to significant business wins. According to Bater[6], the time-based billing operated by professional services industries can be used to develop metrics that demonstrate the value of KM initiatives and resources that save professionals' time. The same applies to task-based billing or even flat fees – i.e. if it takes less time to accomplish the same job, the profit margin will be higher for that job.

Most importantly, it has to be recognised that KM requires long-term investment to achieve a sustainable ROI, so measurement is critical in order to monitor progress. As Wesley Vestal[7] explains, "ROI takes time to gather due to the complexity of understanding the impact that people, process, content and technology have on knowledge sharing, and subsequently the business." As the following chapters demonstrate, KM measurement highlights the significant advantages derived from effective knowledge management that boost the balance sheet of successful KM enterprises and underpin their competitive advantage.

References

1. The 2006 Global MAKE press release. The 2006 global MAKE study was conducted by Teleos in association with The KNOW network: www.knowledgebusiness.com
2. Bair, J., *Making Knowledge Work* (Ark Group, 2004, p.10)
3. Ibid, pp. 49-54
4. Bater, B., *KM in the Legal Profession* (Ark Group, 2005, p.56)
5. Adams, S., 'Practice Makes Perfect' in *Inside Knowledge* (Ark Group, volume 9, issue 4, December 2005)
6. Bater, B., *KM in the Legal Profession* (Ark Group, 2005)
7. Vestal, W., *Measuring Knowledge Management* (American Productivity and Quality Center, 2002)

2. The business case for measurement

ALTHOUGH THERE is no way to guarantee continuous success in business, it is often said that what you don't measure, you can't manage. Therefore, measurement is an essential part of maximising the value and effectiveness of an organisation's KM programme. Establishing its ROI – the value it adds to the company – serves both to establish a clear value proposition to justify ongoing investment in existing and new KM programmes and initiatives, and to identify areas that require improvement. This chapter examines the business case for measuring KM capabilities in order to maximise their contribution to business performance and competitive advantage.

KM's business drivers

In *Making Knowledge Work*,[1] Jim Bair identifies the following business drivers for KM:

- Knowledge sharing and competitive response;
- Innovation;
- Reducing or controlling costs;
- Reducing loss of intellectual assets from employee turnover;
- Increased need to operate globally;
- Compliance

As well as driving KM, these and other context-specific factors also drive business success. Therefore, effective KM makes good business sense. However, developing, implementing and maintaining KM resources and activities that facilitate and sustain knowledge flow, particularly those involving technology and dedicated personnel, requires significant ongoing investment. Measuring the actual and potential contribution of KM in relation to these factors helps to ensure its continuing value both in financial terms and in terms of the organisation's control over its knowledge assets.

The strategic role of KM measurement

KM focuses on leveraging an organisation's knowledge assets to create value for the business, its employees and its customers. Therefore an effective KM programme that achieves a significant ROI must be aligned with the company's business profile, its strategic vision and mission and its critical success factors. As Carl Frappaolo[2] explains in *Next Generation Knowledge Management*, "To satisfy the fiscal reality needs of today's management, we must ask them to give us the hot spots or metrics by which they wish to see an ROI. Why would they invest not only in knowledge management, but in any information handling activity? What issues do they feel need to be addressed to ensure the solvency and competitiveness of the organisation?"

Of course, for many companies, including the case study organisations in part 2 of this report, their market value and competitive advantage depend on maximising the leverage on their knowledge assets and activities. Therefore, the ROI on KM activities is both a key performance indicator and a critical success factor, so continuous measurement is essential in order to monitor progress and drive business performance. Halliburton (see chapter 12) invests in KM programmes only after pilot projects have delivered a significant return. At Fluor (see chapter 10) knowledge is a crucial part of the company's mission, which is to be the premier provider of global, knowledge-based engineering, procurement, construction and maintenance (EPCM) services. At Ricardo (see chapter 16) knowledge flow is critical to the company's service offering, so KM in the form of leveraging knowledge inputs is necessarily a top priority. At professional services firms intangible assets such as expertise, intellectual capital and reputation underpin their business performance and competitive position.

Compelling reasons to measure

As Melissie Clemmons Rumizen[3] puts it in *The Complete Idiot's Guide to Knowledge Management*, "You get what you measure."

In a presentation at I-KNOW in 2004, Gita Haghi[4] of Hewlett Packard made an effective case for KM measurement, stating, "Measurement tells us whether our KM programmes are meeting their targets. Ongoing measurement and analysis will tell us if KM is doing what it is supposed to do. The value and results of KM programmes are only hypothetical unless their effectiveness and their impact on one's business are measured. By defining and publicising our measures, we also encourage employees to behave in ways that contribute to the achievement of KM results." KM measurement:

- Demonstrates how KM supports the organisation in achieving its business objectives;
- Identifies how and where KM programmes and activities add value throughout the organisation;
- Shows the extent to which KM strategies are being implemented;
- Highlights KM deficits;
- Identifies what is and isn't working and where more attention is needed; and

- Communicates KM strategy throughout the enterprise.

The following paragraphs explore a selection of the compelling business reasons underpinning KM measurement.

Justifying continued investment in KM activities

KM activities, particularly those involving introducing and maintaining new technology and enterprise-wide knowledge resources and changing processes, practices and behaviours, are notoriously costly. In today's fast moving, technology-driven, highly competitive business environment, few enterprises have the luxury of allocating resources to internal programmes and initiatives such as KM without being required to demonstrate their value. KM measurement provides the metrics to justify the ongoing costs of knowledge resources and initiatives to management and other stakeholders, who are looking for hard dollar returns. Without measurable success as demonstrated – or at least projected – through cost-benefits analysis, support for KM activities is unlikely to continue. Furthermore, as KM increasingly focuses on connectivity and relevance, it often takes time to deliver a significant return, so progress and outcomes need to be monitored and communicated from the outset.

Gaining leadership buy-in and support

Measurement is critical to gaining and retaining leadership support for KM and ensuring a commitment to the continued allocation of resources. To get the best return on any KM initiative or programme, it is essential that senior managers recognise the value of KM and are prepared to commit resources to it. Pilot projects and specific knowledge-based initiatives that achieve demonstrable returns provide the

Measuring the Value of Knowledge Management

numbers that management need to convince them of the actual and potential benefits.

For example, leveraging global knowledge locally and local knowledge globally is key to Fluor's success (see chapter 10). Its KM programme focuses on connecting people to people and solutions to challenges. At Halliburton (see chapter 12), if managers feel that KM is not delivering they will begin to question expenditures, so all KM projects are required to demonstrate a projected return at the outset.

Managing successful KM implementation

Leading and lagging measures underpin successful KM implementation. Leading measures provide feedback about how KM implementation is going, while lagging measures relate to targets and show in retrospect how KM has affected the business. Measuring by business unit shows whether KM initiatives are inclusive and have the buy-in of the entire organisation, or whether they are confined to particular areas of business. If you don't measure the benefits, how do you know you've got them? According to KM guru David Skyrme[5], KM measurement gives organisations better understanding of the drivers of value and helps them manage and grow these vital assets.

Measuring the benefits and the value added to an organisation by specific tactics, such as communities of practice, expertise finders and self-service learning, helps knowledge practitioners justify the investment of time and money in organising, facilitating and participating in them.

Identifying scope for improvements

Rumizen[6] examines the cost of failing to measure and evaluate KM. She argues that failing to measure means not having the requisite in-depth information to review KM programmes and identify potential improvements. So organisations that fail to measure don't have the metrics to maximise their ROI and are therefore unlikely to secure continued investment in KM. Measurement uncovers where the system isn't working so that remedial action can be taken.

Driving innovation and protecting intellectual capital

As successful companies increasingly focus on research and development, expertise and other intangibles, the correlation between knowledge creation and wealth creation has become more obvious. Consequently, innovation is recognised as a key performance indicator and a significant factor in the market value of knowledge-based enterprises. Innovation metrics link an organisation's knowledge flow and potential to its projected business performance. According to Boston-based Imaginatik Research,[7] the lack of metrics can imperil the very survival of innovation activities within an organisation. By contrast, the right combination of innovation metrics can be used to drive knowledge creation by highlighting the benefits, motivating stakeholders, attracting appropriate resources, diagnosing problems and identifying potential solutions.

Of course, knowledge creation is necessarily an iterative process as one idea or new process leads to another. Intellectual capital expert Karl-Erik Sveiby[8] highlights organisational learning as a key driver of measuring intangibles. "Measuring can be used to uncover costs or value creation opportunities otherwise hidden in the traditional accounts. What is the cost of staff turnover? What is the value of the learning that takes place when staff interact with customers? What is the value creation opportunity lost in having inadequate systems for knowledge management? The learning motive promises the highest long-term benefits."

Measuring and categorising knowledge flow in terms of inputs and outputs creates an organisational knowledge inventory which helps to protect a firm's intellectual capital against, for example, staff turnover and retirement. Communities of practice (CoPs) at Caterpillar (see chapter 9) help the organisation create and retain knowledge by including a wide range of internal and external stakeholders, rather than being limited to the employee population.

Using metrics to drive KM behaviours that deliver measurable results

In order to embed KM throughout an organisation, everyone working within it needs to be aware of the substantial benefits that it can generate. Communicating meaningful metrics encourages the behaviour changes that may be required to achieve the best ROI on KM. For example, best practice replication at Ford (see chapter 11) produces cost savings and quality improvements, but these depend on people participating in CoPs and utilising online KM applications. Quantifying these positive outcomes encourages more participation which in turn increases their ROI enterprise wide. Therefore, measuring the outcomes of KM provides the metrics that drive involvement in KM activities which underpin their ROI. For example, as more people use BAE Systems' virtual university (see chapter 7), the savings to the company in terms of training costs increase, improving the ROI on introducing and running the virtual university.

So, having recognised the business case, how should an organisation put KM measurement into practice? Of course, the best methodology for any organisation will depend on contextual factors, including:

- The profile of the organisation;
- The priority given to KM;
- The level of investment in KM;
- The approach to KM;
- What the organisation is looking for from KM;
- Its KM objectives; and
- The maturity of its KM.

Most organisations benefit from a combination of qualitative and quantitative measures based on lagging and leading indicators related to their particular critical success factors. The following chapter explores a selection of popular KM measurement methodologies.

References

1. Bair, J., *Making Knowledge Work* (Ark Group, 2004, pp.17-20)
2. Ash, J., *Next Generation Knowledge Management* (Ark Group, 2006, p.13)
3. Rumizen, M.C., *The Complete Idiot's Guide to Knowledge Management* (Madison, WI: CWL Publishing Enterprises, 2002, p.207)
4. Haghi, G., 'Measuring Knowledge Management at HP Services Consulting & Integration' (Proceedings of I-KNOW '04)
5. Skyrme Associates website www.skyrme.com
6. Rumizen, M.C., *The Complete Idiot's Guide to Knowledge Management* (Madison, WI: CWL Publishing Enterprises, 2002, p.207)
7. http://www.knowledgebusiness.com/knowledge-business/Templates/ReadKnowledgeLibrary
8. Sveiby, K. E., Methods for Measuring Intangible Assets http://www.sveiby.com/Portals/0/articles/IntangibleMethods.htm

3. Measurement methodologies

IT IS widely acknowledged that it is difficult to demonstrate a hard ROI in respect of KM initiatives. As Wesley Vestal[1] puts it, "It is extremely difficult to create any measure of knowledge sharing that will show an absolute one-to-one correlation between a knowledge-sharing action and a business result. Much like measuring the success of training and development programs, measuring the impact of knowledge sharing requires correlation and some assumption." Despite this, many KM experts and practitioners believe that developing a measurement framework helps managers to make explicit their tacit assumptions about knowledge flow and transfer and the value it brings to their business.

A number of approaches can be drawn upon in order to justify the investment of money, time and effort and measure the effectiveness and the value of KM strategies, tactics and initiatives. This chapter outlines some of the more popular methodologies for assessing the benefits of KM, measuring the success of KM initiatives and evaluating intellectual capital.

KM as a business expense

A straightforward approach is simply to ask what one is getting for one's money. Kingsley Martin[2] has explored some options for measuring the costs of KM and justifying its value. Although these were developed with law firms in mind, they can be applied to any professional services organisation. They also concentrate primarily on calculating the ROI on KM technology. Martin's approach, which is summarised in *KM in the Legal Profession*[3], sets out two main options: cost recovery and cost justification. Cost recovery usually manifests itself as an attempt to quantify usage in pursuit of each client commission and factor the resultant costs into the fees charged. Alternatively, the cost of KM is regarded as a business expense and spread across all commissions in a particular financial year. Cost justification looks for an audit trail leading to an identifiable impact on the bottom line.

Martin advocates a two-pronged approach to measuring the ROI on KM technology projects. He recommends conventional ROI calculations for measuring the hard financial benefits, and applies a cost of information (COI) formula to measure the soft benefits of KM by calculating "the expense of knowledge sharing by comparing the per-document cost of the system to the average rate of document re-use", focusing on "the effectiveness of the investment in generating intellectual capital by measuring the rate at which technology expense is converted into valuable information assets." The inherent difficulties in this approach are causation – the fact that KM technology touches on numerous processes, so its costs and benefits cannot be considered in isolation – and equivalency – in that many of the benefits cannot easily be converted into financial value.

Clare and Detore's six-step KM valuation model

As Martin's approach demonstrates, the problem with attempting to determine the ROI on KM is although both the costs and benefits can be considerable, they can be difficult to pin down. Furthermore, many of the significant benefits of KM, such as increased knowledge sharing and collaboration and better decision-making, are difficult to quantify in financial terms.

Taking these difficulties into account, Mark Clare and Arthur Detore developed a rigorous six-step model for determining the ROI of a proposed KM strategy or initiative. This project-based approach also provides a framework for developing a KM strategy. The process is outlined by Melissie Clemmons Rumizen[4] in *The Complete Idiot's Guide to Knowledge Management* and is summarised below.

1. **Identify opportunities.** Set the agenda by answering three central questions:

   - What do you know as an organisation? How does this knowledge distinguish you in the market place?
   - How can you create more value from what you know?
   - How can you get the knowledge needed to succeed in the future faster than your competitors?

   The output is a preliminary description of how to leverage the organisation's knowledge assets.

2. **Scope the project.** The goal is to identify all the areas of the organisation that will be affected by a proposed KM project, including business processes. This step also encompasses traditional scoping – what's included in the project and what's out of bounds. The output is a high-level model that frames the project in both business and KM terms.

3. **Develop an operational model.** The goal is to create a model of how the KM strategy will be delivered. The outputs include developing an operational model that is detailed enough to make a connection between the knowledge assets and the creation of economic value and to identify value drivers.

4. **Discover value drivers.** The goal is to refine an understanding of the value drivers identified in step 3 and use them to build causal models of how they work through the operational model. The outputs include a revised KM proposal and a knowledge value tree that links the operational impact of the project to its economic value.

5. **Develop valuation framework.** The goal is to understand the value currently being created or destroyed by the operations within the project's scope. This provides a baseline for assessing the impact of the project. The output for this step is a complete framework for valuation.

6. **Test and refine scenarios.** The purpose is to develop a specific scenario for implementation. Outputs include a formal KM project proposal.

Performance measures

Although Clare and Detore's methodology offers a comprehensive approach to measuring the value of specific KM initiatives and strategies, the ultimate objective of KM is to improve overall organisational performance and to support the achievement of core strategic objectives. Therefore, as Rumizen explains, the best long-term way to measure the impact of KM is to link it to key performance indicators and apply a combination of quantitative and qualitative measures to evaluate the benefits of KM activities. The inherent difficulty in this is differentiating the contribution of KM activities from that of other critical success factors.

Measuring the Value of Knowledge Management Chapter 3

O'Dell and Grayson[5] developed a model that attempts to separate the relative contribution of KM to the success of a project or process through a two-pronged approach based on measuring outcomes and activities.

Measuring outcomes connects KM with business performance by evaluating the impact on the business of projects and processes that depend on KM. Relevant outcomes might include cost reductions or quality, productivity or efficiency improvements.

Measuring activities focuses on specific KM activities and their effect on particular projects or processes. This involves tracking how many and how often users access, contribute to, apply and reuse knowledge resources, including participation in communities of practice and interest and other networking activities. The findings of these quantitative measures can be combined with qualitative measures such as employee surveys, with the objective of discovering the attitudes and behaviours behind these activities. The results are set against the costs associated with KM activities and initiatives.

The Balanced Scorecard

One of the most popular performance measurement systems is the balanced scorecard, developed by Kaplan and Norton. As Rumizen explains, this model focuses on factors that help deliver an organisation's overall strategy by linking its core strategic vision and business objectives to four key performance measures.

Financial – How do we look to our shareholders? These measures centre on profitability and other key financial ratios, including return on capital employed and economic value added.

Customer – How do customers see us? The goal is to identify desired outcomes of the business strategy. Key factors are price, quality and response time. Core measures include customer satisfaction, retention and market share.

Internal processes – What must we excel at to succeed? This includes innovation as a leading indicator of financial performance. Kaplan and Norton's value chain model focuses on innovation, operations and post sale service.

Innovation/learning and growth – How can we continue to improve and create value? This focuses on how the company can learn and grow to meet the other three objectives. Innovation, learning and growth are measured as indicators of future performance and can be used to give managers an insight into what KM activities will best deliver their strategic mission, goals and objectives.

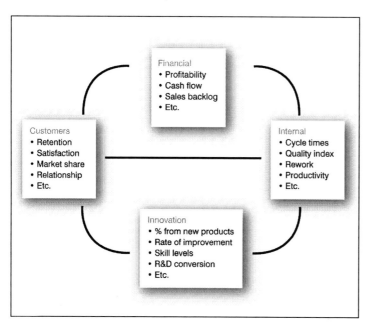

Figure 1: Balanced Scorecard Model
Source: Skyrme Associates[6]

Rumizen identifies this methodology as having the following advantages:

- It includes hard and soft measures. As Rumizen explains, three out of the four balanced scorecard perspectives are non-financial and relate to intangible business drivers;
- It focuses on leading and lagging measures. The first two perspectives, financial and customer, are lagging indicators, while the second two, internal processes and innovation/learning and growth, are leading indicators. Although financial indicators are necessarily retrospective and in the case of KM they cannot provide comprehensive results, they do offer a degree of bottom-line justification for investing in KM;
- It links measurement to strategic business objectives and provides feedback about how well the strategy is performing, driving alignment between KM and the organisation's overall mission, vision and objectives. It also helps to communicate strategy;
- It is flexible and can be applied to all functions at every level of an organisation, so can be used to drive organisational change.

Assessing the benefits of KM

As Bob Bater[7] explains, there are a number of approaches that can be used as feeds for KM performance indicators in an overall organisational balanced scorecard. Approaches to justifying investment in KM fall generally into three broad types.

1. General guides for assessing KM benefits that provide frameworks for stimulating discussion and agreement on what benefits are important to a particular firm and how these might translate into overall business benefits;
2. Attempts to identify the firm's key intellectual capital – i.e. contributes to business outcomes, and implements ways of tracking its value before and after a KM initiative;
3. A wide range of specialist methods focused on specific types of initiatives, such as the value of CoPs.

Skyrme Associates' Benefits Tree

Skyrme Associates' benefits tree model falls into the first category, as it illustrates the interdependencies between different types of benefit. David Skyrme explains how it works: "Many senior executives want a clear understanding of the bottom line benefits of KM before they invest. Typically, a

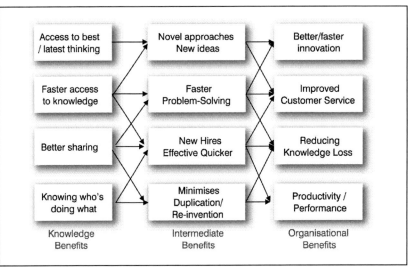

Figure 2: Skyrme Associates KM Benefits Tree
Source: Skyrme Associates

knowledge initiative is an infrastructure project where the cost is visible, but the benefits are diffused throughout the organisation. A benefits tree relates the immediately visible benefits, through a series of steps to those understood by senior executives."

Figure 2 above is an example of a benefits tree, which highlights some commonly found benefits of KM. It is accompanied by the following explanation: "The arrows indicate which benefits lead to higher level benefits. The benefits on the left are those that are the most visible or quantifiable. Those to the right are the result of several factors, including non-KM factors. In this particular tree, three different classes of benefit have been used.

1. **Knowledge benefits** – these are those derived from more efficient processing of information and knowledge, for example, by eliminating duplication of effort or finding relevant information faster.
2. **Intermediate benefits** – these are how the knowledge benefits could be translated into benefits that can be expressed in terms of efficiency or effectiveness. A common example is that best practices databases help to eliminate less efficient operations through transferring knowledge from the best practitioners.
3. **Organisational benefits** – these are the benefits that impact key goals, such as productivity and customer service."

Skyrme Associates adds the following comment: "As a result of such analysis, it is possible to track savings of time in accessing knowledge, through to better customer service by giving them more relevant, validated and timely solutions to their problems. It is quite common to have four or even five classes of benefit. For example, organisational benefits can be divided into two classes, one internal benefits, the other customer or market-related benefits."

Evaluating intangible assets and intellectual capital

As Leif Edvinsson explains in *Next Generation Knowledge Management*[8], the rise in investment in intangibles such as research and development, education and competencies, IT software and the internet has led to a growing interest in measuring – with a view to maximising – the added value derived from leveraging intellectual capital (IC), which includes intangible assets such as management skills, innovation and, of course, knowledge and expertise. Although IC is difficult to quantify and does not appear on the balance sheet, it has a significant effect on hard financial metrics, in particular the net worth of the company. In fact, the most widely recognised IC indicator is the difference between market value and book value. As Karl-Erik Sveiby[9] states on his website, "The difference between a company's market value and book value can be directly attributed to its intangible assets." For companies like AOL and Microsoft, intangibles make up around 90 percent of their market capital. Effective KM must therefore be directed at maximising the return on these intangible assets.

There are many different approaches to IC measurement, which Skyrme Associates divides into four categories:

- Asset – valuing knowledge as an asset, potentially tradable;
- Benefits – focusing on the benefits of a KM programme;

- Baseline – assessing KM effectiveness as a basis for year-on-year comparison;
- Action – focusing on performance measurement.

According to Rumizen, the most popular IC measurement models, a selection of which are outlined below, are based on the balanced scorecard method (which concentrates on performance measurement) and involve identifying indicators or indexes for a range of intangible asset components. These indicators are then reported graphically as numerical scores.

One example is Sveiby's Intangible Assets Monitor, which is based on the underlying belief that people are the key drivers of corporate revenue and links the firm's intangible assets (divided into three categories: external structure, internal structure and competence with further subdivisions into indicators of efficiency and utilisation, stability, and growth and renewal) to its operational strategies.

However, the limitation of this model is that it does not relate an organisation's intangible assets to its financial goals. Other IC models move beyond skills, technology and climate to uncover the activities fuelling competitive advantage and link them to financial outcomes.

The Skandia Navigator, created by Edvinsson and Malone for the Swedish financial services company Skandia, organises 112 universally applicable measures into five categories: Financial, Customer, Process, Renewal and Development, and Human.

Skandia was the first company to produce a corporate annual report on IC, directly linking the value, impact and effectiveness of intangible assets to accounting measures. This approach also includes a time dimension. "Financial measures indicate the past; customer, human and process measure the current performance of a company; renewal and development predict future performance," writes Rumizen. Leif Edvinsson[10], now the world's first professor of IC, explains that IC measurement also relates to future accounting in terms of the projected ROI on innovation capability – a critical success factor for R&D-intensive companies – which is fostered by effective KM. "Future earnings potential could and should be included in future financial flow analyses. To do that, the organisation has to identify and show indicators of the process."

Another model, the Intellectual Capital Index, relates a firm's intangible assets to its market value. It identifies four categories of intellectual capital – relationship, human, infrastructure and innovation – assesses their relative importance and consolidates them into a single index with a view to:

	External Structure	Internal Structure	Competence
Growth/Renewal	Profit/customer Growth in market share Satisfied customer index	IT investments R&D investment	Number of years' education Share of sales from competence enhancing customers
Efficiency	Sales per professional Profit per customer	Support staff % Values	Value added/employee
Stability	% large companies Devoted customer (repeat orders)	Turnover "Rookie" ratio	Professional turnover Relative pay

Figure 3: Sveiby's Intangible Asset Monitor

Measuring the Value of Knowledge Management Chapter 3

Systems	Output	Outcomes
■ Response time ■ Number of downloads ■ Number of sites accessed ■ Dwell time per web page ■ Usabilit ■ Frequency of use ■ Navigation path analysis ■ Number of help desk calls ■ Number of users, frequency of use ■ Percentage of employees using system	■ Usage survey usefulness to help user accomplish tasks ■ Usage anecdotes, with quantitative assessment of how it has contributed to business performance	■ Time saved ■ Money saved ■ Resources saved ■ Percentage of successful output compared to prior to KM

Figure 4: US Department of the Navy KM Measurement Categories

- Showing the strategic impact of changes in intellectual capital;
- Determining which categories were most important; and
- Providing a basis for comparison across different companies and business units.

According to Rumizen, the authors Göran and Johan Roos claim that changes in the index are related to changes in a firm's value, therefore this dynamic model can indicate trends and predict returns as investment strategies shift. However, the apparent simplicity of a single index means that it requires greater interpretation before it can be used in decision-making.

Professor Philip M'Pherson's Inclusive Value Methodology combines financial and non-financial hierarchies of intangibles which are assigned value ratings according to priorities. A computer model determines the overall value rating and tests for areas of risk.

Although IC measurement models produce indices, ranked indicators and hierarchies, they depend ultimately on a necessarily subjective approach because their effectiveness depends on selecting appropriate indicators and ensuring that their weighting genuinely reflects the organisation's strategic priorities and critical success factors. Despite this, IC measurement is increasingly used to demonstrate the value of KM to the overall workings of the organisation and its market value, thereby providing a framework for decision-making, particularly in research and develpment intensive, innovation focused enterprises and professional services firms, whose market position depends on their intangible assets.

The ARC model deployed by Berwin Leighton Paisner (see chapter 8) combines traditional accounting principles with IC measurement to produce an annual KM report which is used to measure year-on-year progress towards KM goals.

Measuring specific initiatives

Although there are many different ways of measuring the return on specific KM initiatives, the approach outlined in a document produced by the US Department of the Navy (DON) and summarised by

Bater[11] in *KM in the Legal Profession* is applicable to most organisations. The DON recommends some 15 general KM measures as well as particular measures specific to certain types of initiative, such as expertise directories and CoPs. As Bater explains, the DON document distinguishes three categories of measurement: systems, output and outcomes. Examples of measures in each category are shown in Figure 4.

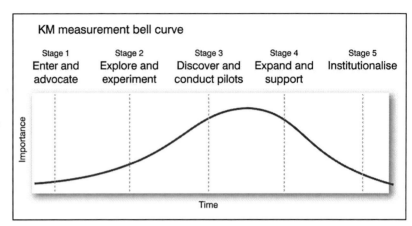

Figure 5: APQC KM Measurement Bell Curve
Source: Bater, B., KM in the Legal Profession (Ark Group, 2005, p.63)

KM maturity models

The right approach for measuring the benefits and success of KM depends on the stage of KM maturity that an organisation has reached. KM maturity models help to develop a framework of measures that are appropriate for different stages of KM implementation. Among the best known is that developed by the American Productivity and Quality Center (APQC) which divides KM into five stages, over which the importance of measurement varies widely:

1. Getting started (enter and advocate);
2. Develop strategy (explore and experiment);
3. Launch KM initiatives (conduct pilots);
4. Expand and support;
5. Institutionalise.

The APQC bell curve illustrated in Figure 5 demonstrates that measurement is not only difficult, but largely irrelevant at certain stages. In the first stage, measurement has little meaning beyond demonstrating the need for KM. In the second stage, the goal should be better appreciation of the potential of KM by management and their support for further development. Possible measures include the number of active sponsors and the level of funding committed to KM. At stage three, however, metrics become crucial to ensure that direct benefit is being perceived as resulting from investing in KM pilot projects. Three types of metric are identified: anecdotal, qualitative and quantitative. The importance of measurement continues into the fourth stage, which builds on the foundations laid by the pilot projects. However, in the final stage, the need to measure KM outcomes gives way to measurement of the business processes which KM supports. The goal is no longer to prove the value of KM, but to indicate continuous improvement. Appropriate measures include demonstrating individual KM behaviours and comparing the organisation's KM practices with those of its competitors.

This chapter has explored some of the best-known methodologies used to assess the ROI of KM – a selection of the growing number of potential approaches. Hopefully, they highlight both the difficulty and the insights to be derived from KM measurement. As Bater argues, in many situations it is accepted that certain factors are crucial despite the fact that their contribution to a successful outcome cannot easily be isolated and measured. He uses an analogy to illustrate this: "Consider the case of a Formula One racing car. Can we expect to identify and measure the specific contribution made to its performance by effective lubrication? The answer of course is 'No'. But we all know that should the oil supply dry up, it will become apparent how important it is."

References

1. Vestal, W., *Measuring Knowledge Management* (American Productivity and Quality Center, 2002)
2. Martin, K., 'Show Me the Money – Measuring the Return on Knowledge Management' (2002), Law Library Resource Xchange: http://www.llrx.com/features/kmroi.htm
3. Bater, B., *KM in the Legal Profession* (Ark Group, 2005, p.47)
4. Rumizen, M.C., *The Complete Idiot's Guide to Knowledge Management* (Madison, WI: CWL Publishing Enterprises, 2002, pp.231-2, 239-249)
5. O'Dell, C. and Grayson, C. J., *If Only We Knew What We Know* (New York: Simon and Schuster, 1998)
6. Skyrme Associates website www.skyrme.com
7. Bater, B., *KM in the Legal Profession* (Ark Group, 2005, p.153)
8. Ash J., *Next Generation Knowledge Management* (Ark Group, 2006, pp.19-27)
9. Karl-Erik Sveiby's website http://www.sveiby.com
10. Ash J., *Next Generation Knowledge Management* (Ark Group, 2006, pp.19-27)
11. Bater, B., *KM in the Legal Profession* (Ark Group 2005, p.156)

4. How to measure: tools and tactics that work

THE FIRST three chapters of this report have outlined the strong business case, and the inherent difficulties, involved in measuring the return on KM. However, as KM activities become embedded into an organisation's business model, it becomes harder to separate their positive impact on the balance sheet from other contributory factors. As Steve Denning[1], business guru and former KM programme director at the World Bank states on his website, "There is thus a measurement paradox: the more the organisation is successful in mainstreaming knowledge sharing as the normal way of conducting the business of the organisation, the more difficult it will be to isolate the impact of any particular actions or expenditures in KM. Nevertheless, the measures of inputs, activities, outputs and outcomes can go a long way to reassure sceptics that the effort to share knowledge is worth it." Having been convinced of the strategic importance of KM measurement, where is the best place to start? This chapter looks at some of the measurement tools and tactics used by leading KM organisations and practitioners to identify the ROI of KM and highlight its impact on business performance.

Link measures to strategy

First, as Melissie Clemmons Rumizen[2] puts it, "Measuring for the sake of measuring is a waste of time – be sure that you're measuring for a purpose." Experts agree that it is absolutely crucial to define the purpose of any KM measurement exercise. The case study organisations in part 2 of this report show that effective KM measurement must be linked to business goals and priorities. Some go so far as including KM in their corporate mission and strategic objectives.

Target value propositions define expectations

Establishing target value propositions helps to define the KM expectations that apply to the business as a whole and to managers and staff at different levels in the organisation. Wesley Vestal[3] summarises a number of KM metrics initiatives in large global organisations employing the following target value propositions:

- Reduce operating costs, improve operational excellence, improve safety (Chevron Texaco);
- Provide faster access to information, improve information management, improve sales leads (Dow Chemical);
- Decrease customer service costs (GE Plastics);
- Create a single global company, reduce cycle time, 'too fast to follow' (Shell);
- Know how: a brand attribute; ability to innovate and execute faster and smarter than competitors (BP);
- Faster revenue growth, lower costs (CapGemini Ernst & Young);
- Revenue growth, industry leadership (IBM Global Services);
- Bring creative new solutions to market faster, shorten the learning curve, lower costs (Best Buy).

Six steps to effective KM measurement

According to Rumizen, the process of developing measures often produces a clearer understanding of how an organisation defines its business goals. She recommends a practical six-step KM measurement process:

- Determine the goals of the measurement exercise – if the initial goals are not sufficiently clear, it will be difficult to measure progress against them;
- Identify the audience for the measures;
- Define the measures;
- Determine what data will be collected and how it will be collected;
- Analyse and communicate the measures; and
- Review the combination of measures.

These and other practical measures are explored in more detail in the paragraphs below.

Set clear parameters

In order to establish KM metrics that demonstrate a clear ROI rather than a soft promise, it is crucial to establish a baseline position before implementing KM programmes and activities. As Vestal puts it, "If you do not know where the starting line is, how can you say what your time is at the finish line?" It is equally important to define the scope of the exercise by setting clear parameters and clarifying what constitutes success.

Mapping KM uncovers meaningful metrics

According to the National Electronic Library for Health (NeLH)[4], a knowledge audit or knowledge mapping reveals the extent and impact of an organisation's KM efforts and identifies where it needs to focus by answering the following questions:

- What are the organisation's knowledge needs?
- What knowledge assets does it have and where are they?
- What are the gaps in its knowledge?
- How does knowledge flow around the organisation?
- What blockages are there to that flow?

Carl Frappaolo[5] of the Delphi Group advocates analysing the findings of an enterprise-wide knowledge audit in the light of the organisation's critical success factors to uncover opportunities to determine and maximise the ROI on KM resources and activities. "Only by the juxtaposition of these two variables can a valid ROI be constructed," he explains, adding that a knowledge audit is the first step to a viable KM strategy.

Knowledge audits and other knowledge mapping tools build a rich picture of where and how KM adds value, and this can be combined with metrics to determine its ROI. Martin Ward of Ricardo (see chapter 16) has created a map of knowledge flow around the company and compiled an inventory of its tangible and intangible knowledge assets with a view to quantifying them and determining their precise contribution to the company's profits. A regular knowledge audit will also uncover any deficiencies in KM which can then be addressed – a continuous improvement process whereby KM becomes self-regulating and self-enhancing, thereby increasing its own value and ROI.

Choose appropriate measures

It's important to avoid scope creep by defining precisely what will be measured and what measurement approach or approaches will be applied. Rumizen emphasises that measures should be:

- **Valid** – they measure what they are intended to measure;

- **Reliable** – they give consistent results;
- **Actionable** – they produce results that can be acted upon.

The choice and number of measures depend on context. Measures need to be relevant to an organisation's business objectives and appropriate to its KM approach, its existing performance measures and the maturity of its KM programme.

Apply/adapt existing measurement systems to KM

The advantage of using established organisational measures, such as key performance indicators and 6-Sigma, to evaluate the return on KM is that managers, employees and other stakeholders will automatically accept their validity. However, if these measures are not sufficient to differentiate the ROI of KM from other factors, this can be addressed by linking additional KM measures to the existing organisational measurement system.

A project-based approach highlights ROI

An effective way of demonstrating a clear ROI on KM is to measure the return on individual KM initiatives or activities by defining the metrics associated with each project. Halliburton (see chapter 12) tracks the progress of individual CoPs using quantitative and qualitative measures – logging the number of users, what benefits they gained from the community, and the financial impact on business results. In respect of specific KM resources such as expertise finders, usage statistics provide the hard metrics while employee feedback uncovers indirect benefits such as faster response times, which improve customer satisfaction and produce financial returns in the form of repeat business.

A similar approach is to link KM expectations to specific goals and to measure the results by business unit. At Ford (see chapter 11), identifying and sharing best practices aimed at improving quality and productivity has achieved substantial enterprise-wide ROI that can be attributed to specific business units. Hewlett Packard Consulting also compares KM and business metrics by business unit and by country with a view to identifying and addressing any deficits that affect business performance[6].

Uncover the stories behind the statistics

Evaluating KM requires a combination of hard and soft measures, as intangible or indirect outcomes commonly have a significant impact on financial results. For example, improved employee engagement due to KM activities facilitates knowledge sharing, which contributes to better-informed decision-making and the retention of knowledge and expertise through reduced staff turnover. Soft measures help to uncover the intangibles behind the statistics. This can be done at various stages of KM implementation via interviews, focus groups, opinion surveys or general requests for feedback. Alternatively, KM-related questions can be piggybacked onto a general employee survey. Petrucciani[7] takes employee input into account as part of the process of developing a KM measurement system, enabling this to be amended in the light of employee feedback.

Don't choose too many measures

Having identified the priorities, focus on measuring what is important. Vestal refers to Einstein having said that he could manage no more than seven variables at a time, so keeping the number of measures below that benchmark probably makes sense!

Review KM measures

The KM maturity models outlined in the previous chapter demonstrate that KM measurement needs be reviewed periodically. Different metrics become important as different factors come into play.

Start small: pilot projects demonstrate ROI and value

Pilot projects create awareness of the potential return on KM activities. In practical terms, it's easier to get management support for a pilot project than to sell them the concept of an enterprise-wide initiative. The findings of a knowledge audit can be combined with scenario planning to identify potential pilots. A successful pilot project provides managers, employees and other stakeholders with proof of the value of investing in a particular KM activity or process. It also reduces the risk of implementing an enterprise-wide programme that doesn't deliver. For example, Motorola implements only those pilot projects that have demonstrated a clear and significant ROI. However, experts agree that it is important not to conduct too many pilot projects as this will compromise their value for money.

Pilot projects also provide indirect value in terms of organisational learning as they enable potential KM initiatives to be tested, assessed and modified in a controlled environment. This value can be captured by following each pilot project with after-action reviews. As Rumizen explains, this US Army technique asks the following questions:

1. What was supposed to happen?
2. What actually happened?
3. Why are they different?
4. What can we learn to do about it today?

Retrospect, a tool developed by BP for evaluating pilot projects, involves intensive after-action reviews being facilitated externally to ensure that an impartial decision is made as to whether a pilot project should be rolled out to the rest of the organisation. It comprises five steps:

- Review;
- Discussion of what worked well;
- Discussion of what could have worked better;
- Decision on whether to recommend continuing; and
- Planning for the future – developing an expansion strategy building on what's been learned from the pilot study.

Although pilot projects produce hard metrics, they should also be combined with measures that recognise potential long-term ROI, which may be exhibited through reducing future timescales on project completions, for example. Furthermore, the larger the investment, the larger the potential return. In *Making Knowledge Work*, Jim Bair[8] argues that the more people and sources of knowledge are incorporated into a KM system, the greater the benefits, so the ROI grows exponentially as KM activities are rolled out enterprise-wide.

Know your audience: communicate meaningful metrics

Successful KM that achieves significant ROI depends on convincing managers and employees at every level of the organisation of its value. Therefore, effectively communicating KM metrics is crucial. The first question to be answered is, "Who needs to know what?" Another important consideration is that different people have different ideas about what constitutes success. Managers who approve the allocation of resources will want bottom-line evidence of a clear ROI. Users of the KM system will want to know how it supports their roles and functions and whether their participation in KM initiatives and activities has been worthwhile. Other stakeholders, including those who develop, implement and maintain the system, will also want to know the impact of their efforts.

Hard metrics convince leaders and shareholders, while soft measures – such as storytelling – evangelise the employee population and get them involved. As Darius Baria[9], head of knowledge management services at Rolls-Royce, put it in an article for *Inside Knowledge*, "Success stories among peers are far more effective at communicating success than, for instance, presentations from KM practitioners trying to sell a concept." Many companies use anecdotal evidence to communicate intangible benefits, such as speedier access to information and expertise into hard metrics such as productivity gains.

Another consideration is the return on the knowledge and expertise which increases an individual employee's value to the company and in the market. The easiest way of evaluating the personal ROI that individuals gain from KM is to ask them – either by conducting interviews as part of a KM measurement exercise or by including relevant questions in a general or specific employee survey. The findings uncover the extent to which KM is embedded into the organisational culture.

Measuring and communicating the personal ROI that individuals can gain from investing their time and energy in corporate KM initiatives incentivises employee involvement in KM activities ranging from consciously exchanging knowledge and information with colleagues, through to active participation in CoPs, to becoming a KM champion. Although there is no consensus on the benefits or otherwise of linking KM measurement to reward systems, KM metrics can also highlight the contribution of individuals, teams and business units to KM activities that enhance business performance.

A practical demonstration of value

David Skyrme[10] suggests a very simple tactic that is guaranteed to overcome the controversy over KM measurement and the difficulties of demonstrating a clear return on KM investments, particularly IT related resources, where costs tend to overrun: the turn-off tactic. "If, for example, there are concerns about investing more in an intranet, simply turn it off for a few days," he says. "The reaction of those who pop out of the woodwork will give you plenty of ammunition for improving it!"

The case studies in part 2 of this report represent practical examples of how KM measurement supports high-performing enterprises in many different industries and sectors, and helps them maintain their competitive advantage in today's fast-paced, technology driven business environment.

References

1. Steve Denning's website http://www.stevedenning.com/measurementknowledgemanagement.html
2. Rumizen, M.C., *The Complete Idiot's Guide to Knowledge Management* (Madison, WI: CWL Publishing Enterprises, 2002, p.208)
3. Vestal, W., *Measuring Knowledge Management* (American Productivity and Quality Center, 2002)
4. NeLH, *Conducting a Knowledge Audit*, available at http://nelh.nhs.uk/knowledgemanagement/km2/audittoolkit.asp
5. Ash, J., *Next Generation Knowledge Management* (Ark Group, 2006, p.14)
6. Haghi, G., 'Measuring Knowledge Management

at HP Services Consulting & Integration' (Proceedings of I-KNOW, 2004)
7. Petrucciani, P., 'Methodologies for identifying knowledge value measurement indicators in a company' (July 2006) http://www.knowledge-board.com/lib/3443
8. Bair, J., *Making Knowledge Work* (Ark Group, 2004, p.54)
9. Baria, D.,'Rolls-Royce: Memories fade; knowledge shouldn't' in *Inside Knowledge* (Ark Group, volume 8, issue 5, February 2005)
10. Skyrme Associates website www.skyrme.com

5. The Superknowledge Declaration

*THE FOLLOWING extracts from 'The Superknowledge Declaration' by **Victor Newman**, present the Superknowledge Framework, an alternative KM measurement approach that considers the relationship between knowledge and power and its impact on measuring the value of KM.*

The most important element in driving an organisation's success is more than the sum of the knowledge in people's heads integrated into its business processes; it is also the ability of that organisation to deploy its knowledge productively. At this point it is worth understanding some basic concepts or knowledge about knowledge (K2) that determine productive mobilisation of knowledge and its realisation as value in the marketplace.

1. **Knowledge is not, of itself, power.**
   The sheer possession of knowledge is insufficient. If we reverse the equation, then it becomes clear that power is not knowledge, and that some major elements are missing. Therefore we could propose that power equals knowledge plus marketing (where marketing in turn, equals delivery and positioning). Unpacking knowledge delivery involves understanding how to compose the knowledge into discrete chunks, manage their sequential delivery and reinforcement. Unpacking positioning involves connecting the knowledge with a perception of crisis in its audience (so that it solves a problem that is generally understood) and managing its timing of appearance and reinforcement.

2. **The value of knowledge is relative and not absolute**, and is determined by the relative availability of competitive alternatives, and the need to manage and exploit the convergent timings for the arrival of the knowledge to ensure that it is useable and relevant.

3. **Things don't happen when we choose not to implement them.** The decision to make something happen is stressful because it implies an open-ended commitment to control known and emergent dependencies to deliver a specific outcome. Sometimes groups make a surface commitment to implement an idea that is undermined by a covert decision to allow failure by not raising and focusing energy on controlling the necessary dependencies.

4. **The key bottleneck to deploying knowledge productively is expert knowledge power.** Your knowledge experts often create positional power by locating themselves at the bottlenecks of strategic decisions and retain positional knowledge power by blocking off rivals or driving them out of the business. Ironically, your organisational hierarchy reflects where your expert knowledge power is, and flattening your hierarchy can mean that you destroy positional knowledge power and end up as a service business.

5. **Your ability to innovate and hence your pace of innovation is determined by the ability of your knowledge experts to create new knowledge and manage its succession into the business.** This in turn, is determined by the boredom threshold of your experts and the ability of leaders to create an environment where existing knowledge has to be deployed into the organisation and replaced by new

knowledge. Knowledge experts need to become inured to the pain of giving up their children to strangers and creating new ones. The positional knowledge power of experts may be an inadvertent product of their lack of training in managing knowledge succession.

It's time for something different, an approach that we might characterise as 'Superknowledge Thinking', an approach that is closer to the style of the knowledge-intensive, SAS operations of the last 20 years that we tend to take for granted. The modern SAS approach is characterised by a keen appreciation of outcomes and a continual evaluation of potential risk and cost. It's time to shift from the mass, conscript knowledge models toward an approach that is primarily focused on delivering high-value outcomes. An approach that is prepared to unpack and understand the prerequisites that need to be managed and to creatively reconfigure these into a value-driven process where the key decisions and their potentially high-value inputs are defined, piloted, embedded and understood. And individuals are highly-trained and exercise personal discipline and initiative.

The study of disaster and incompetence is a fruitful source of potential knowledge. What we do learn from incompetence is the need to pay attention, to explore ambiguity and knowledge gaps and make deliberate investments in exploring and managing the abyss of risk.

This Superknowledge (SK) declaration is a deliberate, experimental train of logic that was the accidental by-product of some reflections on the problem of measuring knowledge investments.

If we begin by defining KM as the deliberate management of knowledge to deliver specific outcomes, and that our interest in the deliberate management of knowledge is in the pursuit of competitive advantage, then the following propositions become possible.

SK1 *If you are seriously interested in realising high-value outcomes, then you need to know which specific knowledge has the potential (if mobilised) to deliver them.*

In other words, building on GiGo (Garbage in/ Garbage out) as the model: specifically, Valuable Knowledge if deliberately introduced into the system of the business, could lead to High Value Outcomes (Vki:HVo). The question we must ask ourselves is: "what do we know, if anything, that has the potential to deliver high-value outcomes?"

SK2 *But you can still be defeated by not connecting the right people with the right knowledge, in the right format at the right time. Especially when they weren't expecting it, and want to resist it because they were not part of the process of creating and building it.*

So the question becomes: who needs to know what in order to make decisions that lead to the delivery of high-value outcomes?

SK3 *Then we probably need to work backwards from high-value outcomes to identify the chain of dependencies which, together, constitute our knowledge mobilisation infrastructure.*

SK4 *We must develop a new knowledge infrastructure, applying the K2 items (knowledge about knowledge) (1)-(5) listed earlier, that is able to identify*

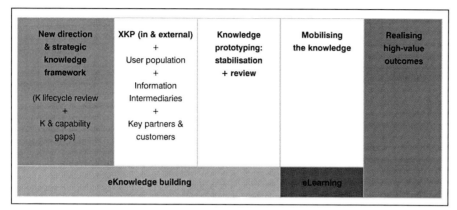

Figure 1: The Superknowledge Framework

and involve the right populations in building new knowledge and mobilising it.

Implications
- SK is a way of thinking about knowledge;
- Building a Superknowledge approach is about connecting the business in a new way by explicitly integrating knowledge, goals and dependencies into a logical flow;
- If we aspire to deliver SK effects, the more likely we are to get them.

Figure 1 above illustrates the Superknowledge framework.

Victor Newman is knowledge activist consultant and visiting professor in knowledge and innovation management: Open University Business School; co-developer of the iCafe strategic conversation technique with David Gurteen and author of 'The Knowledge Activist's Handbook - Adventures in The Knowledge Trenches'. He can be contacted at knowledgeworks@aol.com

6. The value of knowledge doesn't exist
A framework for valuing the potential of knowledge

A great deal of work has been done in the past that seeks to identify how best to measure the value of knowledge and indeed the added value of KM. **Paul Iske** *and* **Thijs Boekhoff** *believe, however, that the real value of knowledge lies in its potential, which is in turn dependent on the context in which that knowledge is used.*

IN THE so-called knowledge economy, intellectual assets have become the most important factor in determining the value of an organisation. Many activities nowadays focus on discovering the Holy Grail of KM: the value of knowledge and the added value of KM. Prominent work in this area includes that done by Sveiby and Edvinsson. However so far it has been difficult to develop quantitative measures that relate knowledge to the economic value of an organisation.

In fact the subject of valuing knowledge can be considered from a more general point of view in which the value assigned is not necessarily a financial one. The 'balanced scorecard' and the Skandia Navigator are examples of measurement methodologies that could be a starting point for developing non-financial measures that help to determine the value of knowledge. However, one question should be considered: why bother measuring at all? Many of the attempts, especially in the US, to develop a framework to measure the intellectual assets of an organisation are driven by the need to develop accountancy standards that equate to those applicable for tangible assets. Such approaches would lead to the formation of a value for knowledge as being the intrinsic property of the organisation. However, in general this cannot be the case.

Consider the process involved in the acquisition of a company, for example. An important stage is the valuation of the target to arrive at a fair price. The target might have knowledge that is complementary to that of the buying party and thus of strategic importance. In this case the knowledge has a high value which will be reflected in the take-over price. Yet if the knowledge is already present in the acquirer's organisation, or it is of no strategic importance, the same knowledge has little or no value. This example demonstrates that the value of knowledge is context-dependent. We can therefore already formulate the main hypothesis of this paper: the value of knowledge is not an intrinsic property but depends on context.

In the remainder of this chapter we will attempt to narrow this statement down and indicate how one could come as close as possible to a workable definition of the value of knowledge. The valuation of intellectual assets remains important in the strategic (management) processes of every organisation. If one asks someone about the most valuable asset of the organisation, the answer is very often: the people, the employees, the staff, etc. However, it seems that this crucial asset is not always being used in the most effective way. We have conducted some research[1] and asked a very simple question: "What percentage of your talent, ideas and experiences do you use in your job (this is not exact science, just select the percentage that first came to your mind)?" The average of the answers (number of respondents 930) is just below 60 percent, with typically a local maximum around 20 per cent and the absolute maximum around 70 per cent (see figure 1). Though it is clear that it is not possible to use the full 100 percent of someone's intellectual capabilities (though there were some people in the age category 50+ who indicated they were using 100 per cent of their brain capacity!), it is clear that a higher return on investment in human capital is feasible! Another conclusion from this research is that there is not much difference between people with different education levels, nor between men and women or between various ages.

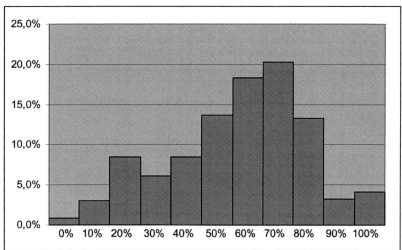

Figure 1: What Percentage of Your Intellectual Capacity Do You Use?

Just for fun: in the Netherlands the total gross wages were, in 2000, about Euro 205 billion. If we accept that knowledge work accounts for at least 50 percent of the total productivity, then every percent of under-utilisation corresponds with a loss of about one billion Euro annually! Of course, this is a very tricky calculation, but it does give an indication of the potential value that is not being realised.

Research from Gartner, for example, revealed that companies that pay explicit attention to the management of intellectual assets achieve anything up to a 30 percent improvement in bottom-line performance.

A framework for valuing knowledge

Knowledge management is a prominent management subject and many books and articles on KM have been published. Some consensus on the basic concepts in the field is evident, but in general the discipline lacks an adequate and accepted language that would allow us to formulate the necessary concepts in an unambiguous way and help us establish a link between theory and practice. Our opinion is that – as stated in the title – knowledge does not have value in itself, but rather in its potential. Instead of the 'value of knowledge' we suggest focusing on valuing knowledge potential.

In this chapter we first offer you a mathematical drill down with which we hope to provoke a lively discussion among those of you who are struggling – as we are – with the question of measurability and the expectation that surrounds it. In the second part we will attempt to bring the discussion back down to earth by exploring the issue in the context of a well-known tool a PeopleFinder (a yellow pages or expert directory) and a new generation of tools that aim to connect workers with experts. So far the potential of these tools is, in our opinion, undervalued, although this is partly because they are so difficult to implement.

A mathematical formulation for knowledge-based value creation

"Whereof one cannot speak one should be silent." These famous words spoken by

Wittgenstein are seldom put into practice. Sometimes, however, we cannot speak simply because we lack the right words or even the right language. In science we see many examples of words or languages that have had to be invented before further progress in a field could be made. For example, in mathematics complex numbers have been introduced as solutions to algebraic equations with some non-real solutions. Complex numbers have proved extremely useful in solving and simplifying various kinds of mathematical and scientific problems.

Though KM is not, and should not be, quite as theoretical and sophisticated from a conceptual point of view, we would probably benefit from the development of a formal language to describe the various stages in the generation distribution (re)usage and evaluation of knowledge.

Obviously we have to start with a definition of knowledge that can be used as a basis for developing the framework. Currently there are probably as many definitions as there are authors, lecturers practitioners and so on. For the purpose of this opinion piece we will use the following definition: knowledge is the combination of insights (past), information (present) and imagination (future), or K=IxIxI, that is being used to make a decision or to select an action by which a situation is changed into a more valuable situation.

There is an implicit value statement included in this definition: the value of knowledge is (part of) the difference between the value of the end-state and that of the original state. In the following we will refer to context as being the original situation, the transition process and the (desired) end-situation. The context also includes the person(s) systems and organisations that are involved in the related decisions and/or actions. Notice that according to this definition knowledge can only add value within a context in particular in the decision-taking step and/or during the action selection. In other words, talking about knowledge is only relevant within a certain context (ie when it is being used). To be able to discuss the value of knowledge potential it has to be stripped from the context where it was generated or used. This is the opposite to some approaches that consider the replacement costs or the cost of generation to be determinant of the value.

Knowledge can be seen as input in a process context. Often it will be available in the form of information embedded in databases, procedures, best practices, frequently asked questions (FAQs), handbooks, personal memory, people's behaviour, etc. The added value can only be obtained if the knowledge is actually used in context. For discussion purposes we propose a formula (see figure 2) that captures the essential features of the knowledge value chain. At the end it enables us to categorise and prioritise properties of organisations' KM activities, and even the value of it all.

The formula in figure 2 thus reads: the total potential value of the knowledge that is stored in the environment equals the sum over all contexts of the probability that this knowledge is related to the context, multiplied by the connectivity that indicates how easy it is to transport the knowledge

$$V_P(K(\Omega)) = \sum_\Gamma \left\{ \pi(K(\Omega), \Gamma) \rho(K(\Omega), \Gamma) \alpha(K(\Omega), \Gamma) V(K, \Gamma) + \sum_i \left[V_P(\mathbb{L}_i^\Gamma(K(\Omega), \Omega_i)) - I(\mathbb{L}_i^\Gamma(K(\Omega), \Omega_i)) \right] \right\}$$

Figure 2: Formula for the Valuation of Knowledge Potential

from the environment to the context, multiplied by the activation coefficient that indicates how easy it is to activate the knowledge (to use it) in the context, multiplied by the added value that is achieved within the context. Furthermore, added value is obtained by learning, which means generating new knowledge in context (as a consequence of the knowledge that has been used in this context) that can be stored in an environment at the expense of an investment.

The total value of all knowledge potential in the organisation is then represented by the equation shown in figure 3.

We can summarise the elements in the first formula that need to be discussed in more detail as:

- Knowledge relevance indicator – the level to which knowledge is considered relevant for the business (processes) and the level to which business issues lead to new knowledge;
- Knowledge connectivity factor – the level to which it is possible to transport knowledge from an environment (source) to the context (work situation/business process);
- Knowledge activation factor – the level to which it is possible to activate knowledge (to use it) in a specific context;
- Added value in context – the level to which knowledge has added value (has been useful) in a specific context;
- Knowledge capturing and learning – the level to which new knowledge is generated in a specific context (as a consequence of the knowledge that has been used in this context) which can be stored in a specific environment at the expense of a specific investment.

$$V_P(K) = \sum_\Omega V_P(K(\Omega))$$

Figure 3: The Value of Knowledge Potential

Note that it is clear from the first formula that if one of the factors is zero, there is no value added irrespective of the value of the other parameters. Quantitative insights into the environmental parameters that determine the value of the factors in the formula will help to optimise the return on investment of knowledge-related projects. In general, one should focus on the smallest parameter (the weakest link) to achieve optimal improvement.

For the purposes of this chapter we will describe our experience in the case of a PeopleFinder implementation to indicate how these elements can help us to structure discussions as to the value of knowledge, and in particular the added value of KM. A PeopleFinder is an automated system to search for and locate people with expertise and experience relevant to a given project (competency profiles).

The end result in many KM system implementation projects is usually an infrastructure or information communications technology (ICT) environment through which information is pushed to the user. The internal debate is always about the best way to attract the user to the system in order to encourage people-to-machine interaction and thus value to the business.

Knowledge relevance indicator

The great advantage of PeopleFinder-type systems is that the link between knowledge and the originating context is clear. In other words, the relevance factor between knowledge and the specific context can be quite large. This will be even more evident

Measuring the Value of Knowledge Management

in the next generation tools in this area which are expert-locating systems based on questions and answers. A good example of a Q&A-based tool is the website: www.askme.com. Currently there are several suppliers of AskMe-type applications for use within organisations and within networks of organisations and their partners/customers. Also, Google and Yahoo have recently started initiatives to use Q&A services to access the 'wisdom of crowds'. We believe these tools can add a great deal of value and we have seen some interesting business cases for the implementation of such systems with a reasonably well-justified ROI calculation. Further, the use of advanced personalised tools such as portals and applications like Autonomy helps to increase the probability that relevant knowledge is transferred to the context.

Some case examples demonstrate the importance of the knowledge relevance indicator in the past. For instance, 3M initially invented glue that could have been dismissed as 'useless', but a newly created context allowed the hugely successful Post-It notes to be invented.

Knowledge connectivity factor

Standard KM solutions hardly seem to solve the problem of how to transform information push into information pull through the detailed analysis of people's preferences and needs in knowledge-based working processes. It is our opinion that this issue directly relates to the connectivity factor: the exchange between two (or more) persons, as well as the exchange between these workers and the system. Regarding the former, certain fundamental questions need to be answered: what is the organisational (physical) distance? Are there any language barriers or differences? Do they have a relationship (do they know each other? Is there a networking effect?). Are there cultural, including time and compensation scheme constraints?

Research result from the Delphi Group has shown that up to 20 per cent of an employee's time is spent on re-discovering knowledge that was already present somewhere else in the organisation. This is an indication that in most organisations the product of the knowledge relevance indicator and the knowledge connectivity factor is small.

Knowledge activation factor

ICT can be of great value to an organisation, in particular web-based technologies. But the main objective of ICT should, in our opinion, always be to strengthen the interaction between people. The effective and efficient exchange of knowledge depends not only on the ability to transfer, exchange and communicate but also on the ability to understand, accept and leverage. This latter ability is reflected in the knowledge activation factor.

The effective exchange between two persons must be measured according to the presence of trust, communication skills, language (barriers), motivation (to send and to receive), the prevalence of Not-Invented-Here syndrome and (shared) mental models. The success of a PeopleFinder depends heavily on these issues. This seems to be an unmanageable set of factors but explicit (peer or management) attention increases the activation factor. Also, the effective and efficient interaction between systems and individuals can be measured: the way you develop a user-interface, the context-suitable formulation (including language) and the way you introduce the application will lead to measurable increased motivation and usage.

Added value in context

Search results and actions taken upon those results indicate the way knowledge has been of use in the business process. The PeopleFinder allows professionals to locate colleagues with relevant expertise and experience for a given project. The level to which knowledge has had added value (has been useful) in a specific context should be derived from the experiences of these users. The result of the evaluation of the PeopleFinder and its effect on the project team, and thus on the business, is called added value in context. In practice this means that the added value of a PeopleFinder tool is often measured on an anecdotal basis.

Knowledge capturing and learning

Humans possess a great deal of tacit knowledge – we know more than we can say and share. The organisational challenge is to remove the barriers and train people to tap into this knowledge in order to create stronger more innovative companies. It requires leadership skills to attract, train and retain talented and motivated people. It requires vision to guide and coach talent towards collaboration and teamwork. Most learning programmes in companies address content structure and procedures but neglect the context in which these programmes reside. Competence and learning depend on knowing where to find, and how to reuse, the right resources to get the job done. The PeopleFinder facilitates serendipity, and by offering the opportunity to be lucky it is possible to facilitate action learning.

Summary conclusion and next steps

Value does not lie in knowledge itself. The real value lies in the potential of that knowledge and thus in:

- The ability to identify and remove blockages between individuals, and in the system, that hinder interaction;
- The ability of knowledge workers to find what they are looking for and, indeed, through serendipity, what they do not know they are looking for;
- The ability to reuse the knowledge through smart 'packaging';
- The courage and pride of workers to show, communicate and sell their knowledge via personal and digital channels;
- The creativity to identify new contexts in which knowledge is relevant, together with the ability to realise these contexts in the organisation – these are in fact the essentials in the innovation process.

The main conclusion of this article is that one should speak of the value of knowledge potential rather than the value of knowledge. The value added is dependent on the identification of the transfer to, and the activation of, knowledge in the various contexts where that knowledge is being used. The value of knowledge therefore is not the intrinsic property of an organisation, but is dependent on the environment and the objectives of the measurement.

Most organisations focus their KM (ICT) programmes on knowledge transfer and thus on the knowledge connectivity factor. We believe that more emphasis should be put on the knowledge relevance indicator which is directly related to choosing a 'pull' strategy rather than a 'push' strategy. Finally, the knowledge activation factor deserves closer attention, since this determines the actual realisation of the value and is influenced by complicated environmental parameters which are often related to human and cultural influences.

We, the authors of this chapter, are working on making the qualitative relationships described above between the elements in the formula and the environmental parameters more quantitative. This will help in the assessment of the key value drivers and the most efficient and effective ways to realise the potential value of knowledge. We hope that this chapter will spark interaction with our peers, so that together we will be able to take the next step in demystifying the true value of knowledge and make more transparent the return on investments KM activities have to offer.

Reference
1. P.L. Iske, Survey conducted in the Netherlands in 2004.

Paul Iske is senior vice president and advisor, Knowledge Management, Innovation and Entrepreneurship at ABN AMRO Bank. Furthermore, he is a freelance consultant in these areas. He can be contacted at: paul.iske@knocom.com

Thijs Boekhoff is co-founder of Squarewise (http://www.squarewise.com). He can be contacted at: boekhoff@squarewise.com

7. E-learning and know-how within BAE Systems

Richard West explains how investing in people development, collaboration and organisational learning online via the company's Virtual University has generated substantial ROI for BAE Systems.

BAE SYSTEMS, the largest aerospace and defence company in Europe, has annual sales of around £14 billion, designing, manufacturing and supporting military aircraft, surface ships, submarines, space systems, radar, avionics, communications, electronics, guided weapon systems and a range of other defence products. With 100,000 staff speaking six languages across 26 divisions in more than 110 sites, BAE Systems has been focused on maximising the intellectual assets of its engineers, scientists and other professionals since the late 1990s.

The rapid pace of market and technological developments in the defence and aerospace industries have required the development of new capabilities and partnerships, new innovative ways of working, and greater organisational agility in responding to the needs of customers and marketplace.

A cornerstone of the company's approach to addressing these challenges has been its ongoing investment in organisational learning and the development of its people, as reflected in the People Value, and the investment made in the company's Virtual University (VU).

BAE Systems set out to create a learning organisation that would enable employees to benefit from all of the company's experts around the world and the terabytes of information stored in countless data repositories. The VU, built on "University in a Box" (UIB) Autonomy/Gatewest New Media technology, initially set up as a portal to enable more intelligent search and retrieval of information, has cut the time that employees spend looking for information by 90 percent and saved in excess of £65 million.

BAE Systems' philosophy is different to many other organisations, where training is often in the domain of HR professionals with a limited budget to dish out after appraisals every six months. BAE Systems appreciates that employees are learning every day, as they come across new challenges, and work with new people and projects. BAE Systems wanted a system that gave employees access to people and knowledge, not just access to information. The VU forms one of four pillars of BAE Systems as a learning organisation. It is the underlying infrastructure, which supports people, process and content.

The VU is a gateway to know-how; a dynamic library of information that can be accessed by individuals from across BAE Systems. The VU plays a major role in collecting and making available best practice and examples of excellence from across the company. It has become a conduit for good ideas that might otherwise never be shared company wide.

Underpinning the VU strategy is a scalable IT infrastructure designed to deliver organisational learning and know-how company wide and cope with numerous legacy computer systems and complex networks. It was clear from the VU's launch that if the company Intranet had not already been in place, the VU would have had to create it. E-learning and web technology were the only rational solution to creating affordable access to a continuous learning environment for over 100,000 employees, working at over 60 sites across the UK alone, and many more abroad.

Every employee now has access to the VU and its e-based services from a desktop computer or by visiting the nearest Learning Resource Centre. The VU and its Integrated Development Portfolio receives over 22,000 hits a day and remains the most popular site on the Intranet.

Though important, courses are not enough. The VU's thinking was that, to truly drive competitiveness through learning, access to wider sources of learning – such as best practice, know-how, research and even expertise, personalised to an individual's or team's needs, available at the right time – would be needed. Such thinking was reinforced by a significant drive from the Chief Executive to obtain more return on the investment the company had made in its intranet.

The VU's aim was to provide employees with the learning, know-how or information that they sought, where they could simultaneously be offered a customised opportunity to be alerted in the future to what they did not know, but would want to know.

The VU has now pioneered the deployment of its Intelligent Learning Portal (UIB) via a three-tiered approach. First, employees can search across organisational sources such as the intranet, shared drives, learning, and best practice databases as well as premium news sources and people sources. This intelligent search and retrieval receives over 18,000 web hits a day.

Second, individuals can enter a particular website centre of excellence (such as Procurement, Air Systems, Manufacturing, Engineering, Customer Solutions) and be networked immediately into relevant opportunities for educational development, vacancies, potential mentors and links to complementary centres of business excellence and job placements across the company.

The third tier is the ability to create a virtual and global network of people, bringing together 'colleagues' who are asking the same questions or seeking a common answer. These are all potential knowledge brokers. The full integration, exploitation, and leverage of the selected databases, along with the know-how emerging from individual's local and global experiences in diverse businesses, are the strategic goals of the VU in its knowledge brokering role.

Utilising this smart retrieval technology has been a quantum step forward. But achieving the ultimate business performance requires can-do attitudes and a willingness to share best practices, to overcome the barrier of any 'not-invented-here' syndromes.

The VU approach has also been used for training with Desktop Re-life, an enterprise-wide IT upgrade of 100,000 PCs with Windows XP, including 40 new desktop applications. The cost of rolling out classroom-based training for just Microsoft Outlook in 2003 was in excess of £2 million, based on tutor, classroom and incurred costs due to late cancellations, 'no shows' and rescheduled sessions. The Desktop Re-life project used the VU to enable people to find training courses, refreshers on specific things like creating Pivot tables in Excel, identify local IT experts who were close by for coaching and access best practices from Microsoft, in their own time. Subsequently, the approach was awarded a Chairman's Award for Innovation, with estimated savings in excess of £7m.

The VU's edge technology implementation directly supports the VU's overall strategic direction and through this blend of technology, and supporting processes such as Best Practice Detectives, the Chairman's Award for Innovation and the Best Practice Forum, the company can already point to over £65 million pounds worth of savings through Best Practice Transfer and Collaboration and for BAE Systems, it only took seven months to see a return on investment. The long-term benefits are anticipated to be in excess of £150 million.

The VU powered by 'University in a Box' makes it quicker and easier to find people and knowledge in order to share best practices, avoiding duplication of work and re-using solutions across the company, and learning to use existing knowledge.

Additional value has been delivered to external partners and joint ventures, as well as industry bodies and Universities through sharing best practices across the enterprise.

Using the VU, BAE Systems has created a place that anyone can go to in order to access knowledge held within the organisation, share best practices on a global scale, and bring people together.

Richard West is Head of Organisational and e-Learning at BAE Systems. He can be contacted at richard.west@baesystems.com

8. A value judgement: Demonstrating the worth of knowledge management

In 2005, law firm Berwin Leighton Paisner won an e-LOTIES award for its intranet-based know-how tool, the KITs. **Lucy Dillon** *describes the firm's approach to measuring and assessing the value of KM in a legal environment.*

The concept of demonstrating value in knowledge has been a recurring theme for knowledge managers for a number of years. As KM has increasingly become a business imperative for many law firms, the need to demonstrate a return on the significant investment firms are making has become more relevant. However, the reality of how to achieve this has not been easy to grapple with.

This article will examine some of the challenges that face anyone trying to adopt measures to demonstrate the value of KM initiatives, and issues to consider when establishing an appropriate methodology. It will then outline three practical models particularly applicable to the legal environment, which can be adapted to interpret and measure data to analyse the benefits of a KM programme.

Differing approaches to measurement

The difficulty, recognised by many management writers, with trying to assess the financial benefit of KM activities has created two opposing views:

1. There are those who adopt the 'you can't see it, so you can't measure it' approach, which validly recognises the difficulty of trying to demonstrate, in numerical terms, a real ROI on an intangible asset, such as knowledge. This school of thought acknowledges the fact that many have tried to do this unsuccessfully and has therefore concluded that the investment of time and effort is not worthwhile: the quantifiable benefit is simply too uncertain;

2. There are those who have developed tangible outputs and metrics to demonstrate the added value of KM initiatives. Such metrics are increasingly becoming a management imperative. The difficulty with this approach is that statistics are a very blunt instrument with which to measure the benefits of intangible assets.

The right answer must be a combination of these two opposing views. Metrics are essential in the context of KM, but they are notoriously difficult to interpret. If they are to be valuable, they need to be tied in with softer measures that assist in better understanding them.

Some challenges

Some specific challenges await knowledge managers in trying to set up measures for their discipline. For example:

- Traditional accounting practices are meaningless: typical auditing principles apply to tangible assets, and the value of a firm's intellectual capital is not yet measured in any systematic way.

However, this is a developing area for auditors as the focus turns towards the 'knowledge economy'; goodwill and intellectual property rights are good examples of value being attributed to intangible assets;
- Benefits from KM activities are blended with many other management disciplines. For example, the benefits of a more efficient business process could be claimed to be a result of better training (HR), faster desktop applications (IT), more appropriate clients (marketing) or more efficient transfer of knowledge; and they may all be right. As knowledge permeates all law firm activities, extracting and isolating its true value is difficult;
- There is no such thing as 'one size fits all': KM metrics will be different for each and every organisation, as they should be linked to that organisation's specific strategic objectives;
- In a profession where knowledge is often still perceived as an instrument of power, any data extracted relating to its growth is often patchy or even misleading.

Initial considerations

For those setting up a series of performance measures, or reviewing existing ones, there are a number of initial considerations:

- Identify the business need: it is much easier to demonstrate how KM adds value in the context of the achievement of a business objective. Knowledge management should underpin a firm's strategy. It is useful to ask practitioners themselves to articulate what will help them achieve their business goals — it promotes ownership of the initiatives and they will be able to help measure where the impact is being felt;
- Take a snapshot of where you are: this is simple, but is often overlooked in the desire to move forward. Having a reference point to compare back to is essential;
- Get the metrics right: there will initially be an element of trial and error in the selection of the metrics, so you should remain flexible. The key is not to have too many metrics for each indicator, and to keep them simple: a good rule of thumb is three or four metrics for each indicator;
- Action the results: you must be prepared to act on the results, even when the outcome demonstrates that an investment of capital and time has not lived up to expectations. You should be prepared to salvage what you can, learn from the experience and move on;
- Manage expectations: not just your own, but those of your management team and your knowledge workers. Measures cannot be interpreted overnight as time is required for patterns to emerge. At Berwin Leighton Paisner, we took many measures at the launch of our intranet, some of which for the first year looked fairly meaningless. However, looking back over the whole 12-month period, the data fell into some clear patterns, which enabled us to make changes and adapt our development to meet the needs of the users.

Three suggested methodologies

The following three measurement tools are particularly well adapted for use in a legal, KM context:

- List of key performance indicators (KPIs);
- ARC 'goals and themes' (explained below);
- Balanced scorecard.

Measuring the Value of Knowledge Management Chapter 8

List of KPIs

The British Standards Institute (BSI), in its 'Guide to measurements in KM'[1], conducted a survey among a series of (non-legal) knowledge organisations to establish a list of the most important objectives. These were:

- Increased customer satisfaction/value;
- Better employee attitude/ morale/ involvement;
- Cost reduction/savings;
- Better time to market;
- Increased sales effectiveness;
- Higher number of communities of practice;
- Increased new product sales;
- Higher number of KM initiatives;
- Reduced employee turnover;
- Amount of know-how on the system;
- New business initiatives;
- Commercialisation of knowledge products.

In any knowledge-intensive organisation, it is useful to split such metrics into quantitative and qualitative measures, as different management approaches are required for each:

- **Quantitative measures**: these are numeric metrics and will give an insight into the maturity and effectiveness of systems (see inset for some examples). These are simple to collate as they are within the knowledge manager's control, once the audit mechanisms have been developed by the IT department. The benefit of such measures is that they are simple to read, and deliver a powerful message. The downside is that they are susceptible to multiple interpretations and, to make the meaning clear, they often require the back-up of softer qualitative data;

- **Qualitative measures**: these are based on feedback and interpretation and will give an indication of the way KM efforts are being perceived, and of the reputation of the knowledge systems (see inset). These measures need to be collated alongside the quantitative measures, to provide a context to the otherwise hard data. Qualitative measures can be obtained through feedback and survey; stories are a very powerful tool and will give far greater insight into performance than bare figures alone.

ARC model

This is a model outlined by Nigel Courtney of Courtney Consulting at a recent KM conference[2], and provides a useful guide for year-on-year reporting on KM initiatives. ARC is an Austrian technology-research organisation, operating as a public/private partnership. Its mission is to create innovation in industry. Since 1999, it has published an annual report, which includes outputs based on a model. ARC's model is based on a number of defined 'knowledge goals', the performance of which is measured across the five 'intellectual capital themes'. These outputs are analysed and commented upon in the report. ARC has observed that, as a direct result of its annual report, it has been able to secure more project revenue from the private sector, making it less reliant on public funding.

I have adapted the model for the legal sector. An annual report based on these goals and themes is straightforward to produce. The benefit of this model is that it ensures that each resource is considered and, where appropriate, used in the achievement of the knowledge goals.

It promotes innovation in KM service delivery by encouraging knowledge managers to look strategically at the resources available.

The use of this model provides the measures. An analytical report will be required as well as an overall interpretation for each goal. This will include:

- A numeric report providing results for each goal;
- A narrative report providing an interpretation of the numbers;
- An indication of whether the targets have been met and a year-on-year comparison. Please note the 'smiley' as a simple but effective graphic indication of achievement.

Balanced scorecard

This model was developed in the early 1990s by Dr Robert Kaplan (Harvard Business School) and Dr David Norton[3]. Its aim is to provide a clear indication as to what companies should measure to balance the financial perspective. It enables organisations to clarify their strategy and translate it into action. On the website of the Balanced Scorecard Institute, Kaplan and Norton are quoted describing the innovative approach of the balanced scorecard: "The balanced scorecard retains traditional financial measures. But financial measures tell the story of past events, an adequate story for industrial age companies for which investments in long-term capabilities and customer relationships were not critical for success. These financial measures are inadequate, however, for guiding and evaluating the journey that information-age companies must make to create future value through investment in customers, suppliers, employees, process, technology and innovation."

The balanced scorecard has proved popular with law firms in a number of management functions, and has been particularly effective in the context of intangible assets, where financial measurement is not only difficult but also generally meaningless.

It allows managers to look at the firm's vision from four perspectives (financial, client, learning and growth, and internal business processes), the non-financial perspectives complementing the financial measures. These clearly need to be adapted for the KM context (for example: 'financial' as a perspective is not always meaningful, whereas 'efficiency' may be better). For each perspective, the following metrics need to be identified:

- Objectives: where do you want to get to?
- Initiatives: how are you going to get there?
- Measures: how do you know you are progressing towards your destination?
- Targets: how do you know when you have arrived?

Each metric is associated to a question to ensure that the tasks are identified through a systematic and consistent thought process.

One of the major benefits of the balanced scorecard is its flexibility. It is infinitely adaptable, not only within many industry sectors and management disciplines, but also within different management levels.

Demonstrating value

This case study has set out a number of steps to demonstrate how KM is bringing value to your firm.

The process to adopt could be along the following lines:

Measuring the Value of Knowledge Management   Chapter 8

> **Suggested metrics for the KM function in a law firm**
>
> **Quantitative:**
> - System-user statistics;
> - Hits on a website;
> - Use of a precedent;
> - Queries raised and responded to;
> - Training events prepared/attended;
> - Length of time devoted to certain activities.
>
> **Qualitative:**
> - Ease of access;
> - Speed of document production;
> - Quality of document production (that is, fewer mistakes);
> - Ease of location of an expert;
> - Feedback on user satisfaction;
> - Confidence in the systems (success stories).

- Identify the firm's business objectives;
- Articulate how KM can support their achievement;
- Define measures of value for KM activities;
- Use them;
- Report on how these are adding value.

Demonstrating that KM has a positive impact on the achievement of business objectives will make the process of seeking further investment for knowledge initiatives easier to manage.

References
1. British Standards Institute 'Guide to measurement in knowledge management', BSI 2003
2. Nigel Courtney's presentation at the Ark Group conference, 'Demonstrating the value of knowledge management', March 2003
3. Balanced Scorecard Institute: http://balanced-scorecard.com.org

Lucy Dillon is director of knowledge management at Berwin Leighton Paisner. She can be contacted at lucy.dillon@blplaw.com

9. Collaboration and beyond

Caterpillar's Knowledge Network incorporates some 2,700 communities of practice and almost 40,000 users, many of whom work in partner organisations rather than in Caterpillar itself. **Reed Stuedemann** *describes the evolution of a truly collaborative network, explaining just how the company is realising an ROI of over 700 percent in some communities.*

CATERPILLAR IS a large, globally dispersed company, involved in many different products and services. Like many other companies, Caterpillar will see a significant number of its most experienced employees retire in the next few years. Leveraging our intellectual capital has therefore never been more important.

We believe the best way to leverage these assets effectively is to enable our employees as continual learners. Our knowledge-sharing mission is to provide efficient, reliable and easy access to knowledge, and enable collaboration with others across the value chain for the purpose of improving performance. The Knowledge Network (KN) was developed to help address these needs.

The KN is a web-based strategic business asset, developed internally at Caterpillar, delivered via the internet. The KN leverages the intellectual capital of Caterpillar and its value chain by providing collaborative space and access to expertise through communities of practice. Our communities are groups of people with a common interest working together to improve performance. They cross business-unit, geographic and value-chain boundaries, and can range in size from small teams to thousands of people. The KN includes Caterpillar employees, retirees, dealers, customers and suppliers.

History and evolution of the KN

The KN was formed in 1998 at Caterpillar's Technical Center as a way to share lessons learnt and leverage technical knowledge. Knowledge Network users quickly recognised that collaborating and learning from each other was a key factor in the ongoing success of our business units.

Being an integral part of continual learning, the KN was transferred to Caterpillar University in 2001. However, non-technical users found the tool unwieldy and difficult to use. Therefore, early that year, the National Center for Supercomputing Applications worked with Caterpillar to identify potential usability barriers that were limiting people's ability to collaborate and participate in communities of practice. The primary barriers identified in the study were the fear of embarrassment by not knowing how to use the tool and a more general lack of computer skills. This information was combined with the results of internal focus-group studies to redesign the system completely for improved usability and functionality. The redesigned system was tested in Caterpillar University's usability lab, modified based on the results, and re-tested until we had a very intuitive and user-friendly system.

Today, users report that the KN is easy to use. The KN is now widely accepted by even non-technical employees. In addition, online help was developed to answer frequently asked questions.

Value-chain collaboration

At the same time as the redesigned KN was being rolled out as an internal collaboration tool, we were receiving requests from our dealers and customers that were looking for a way to collaborate with Caterpillar.

In March 2002, a pilot of the KN was made available on the internet for our dealers to join select communities of practice. These pilot communities were organised around committees and work groups that were already working together. The Knowledge Network allowed them to improve collaboration by increasing the speed, quality and acceptance of their work. The pilot programme also gave the KN team the opportunity to create a KN interface for the entire value chain.

Several system modifications were made in preparation for extending the KN across our value chain. During the pilot, all community names and entry titles were displayed in the community structure, as well as the search results, even though users were not given access to all communities. For the final roll-out, this was modified so that non-Caterpillar people would only be able to see the community's names and search results to which they had access. In addition, Caterpillar personnel see the complete list of all communities, with a warning symbol by a community security profile if that community is open to external personnel.

An extensive disclaimer agreement was developed by Caterpillar's legal department and added to the KN for non-Caterpillar users. All external users are required to accept the agreement before being given access to the KN.

In July 2002, the production KN system was made available across the internet. We currently have dealers, suppliers and customers involved in our communities of practice, as determined by each community manager. The acceptance of the KN by our value-chain partners has been extremely positive, and quick to show results. It has proven to be an effective tool to convert win-lose situations into win-win opportunities.

Growth rates

From 12 communities in January 1999, we now have over 2,700. We anticipate that this rate of growth will slow, as many of the business-process-related communities have now been established. However, we continue to create more project-related communities that will have a finite life.

The number of new users continues to increase dramatically, as dealers, customers and suppliers become involved. We currently have over 37,000 registered users, 25,000 of whom are Caterpillar employees. It is expected that, at the current pace, Caterpillar employees will be the minority among KN users within a year or two. The Knowledge Network team includes one programmer and four knowledge-sharing marketing and support personnel. The team is assisted by colleagues from each of the major business process areas in establishing communities and training participants in their respective areas. The KN is now the prime source of information for many areas of the corporation.

The KN in action

The KN is used for many things. Some of the more common uses include a place to store information, capture lessons learnt, solve problems and identify/locate experts, and as a better means of quickly integrating new people into their job. It is also used to support and facilitate face-to-face meetings. It allows people across our value chain to provide input and gain feedback from all parts of the globe on issues with which they are involved on a daily basis. The KN provides an environment that enables people to take risks, drive innovation and achieve higher-quality results faster than would otherwise be possible.

The KN communities of practice are structured according to a taxonomy that is based on our business processes. It has been very important to define the scope of our communities of practice based on the business needs of the members. Our communities are structured so they align with the day-to-day activities of their members; their involvement must help them accomplish the tasks needed to do their jobs. A community of practice may be a group of people working on a project with a limited life, or a group involved with a business function that goes on indefinitely. As a rule, the more specific the community purpose, the more value it will provide for the members. At Caterpillar, CoPs with a broader scope have not proven to be particularly successful.

Community roles

There are several different roles that people can play within a community. Every community has a community manager who is responsible for the maintenance and upkeep of their community. Maintenance includes the periodic review of content and community participants. The manager plays a critical role in deciding on appropriate content, and should be highly engaged with other users. The manager also serves as a role model for community participants. They need not be the person with the most knowledge or experience, but they do need to be someone who is recognised as being chiefly concerned with the community's common interest. Good communications skills are an asset managers must have in order to be effective. Selecting and training community managers is an area that we will dedicate more resources to in the future.

In addition to keeping the information in the community up to date, managers are responsible for identifying experts for their community. Experts need to be extremely knowledgeable in the subject matter the community is based around. The KN allows a manager to include a description that explains the expert's skill set as it relates to that community. The expert's description is a searchable field, and the KN is considered to be a reliable source where people can go to locate talent. This enables people to locate knowledge and expertise, as defined in the community of practice, independent of their job title or position. A person may be designated as an expert in multiple communities of practice and have a different description in each one, based on the role they play in that community. Experts cannot leave a community of practice unless the community manager removes them as a designated expert within that community.

In addition, managers may, or may not, have delegates – people who assist the manager with the community managerial duties. Delegates have the same authority as the manager and run the community when the manager is travelling or otherwise unavailable. We recommend that a manager chooses at least one delegate to assist them.

Members of each community are people who are interested in the subject matter, but not recognised as experts. They will, however, gain status and recognition by contributing to the community. Members receive e-mail notification whenever something is posted to the community, and are able to join or cancel their membership at any time.

Security issues

A Caterpillar web-security ID is required to enter the system. This allows community managers to control access to their community, as well as to individual entries in their community, based on the electronic identification. Access to a community is defined in one of three ways: it can be granted based on affiliation (such as 'employee' or 'supplier'), by organisational code, by name, or by any combination of these three factors. Anyone who tallies with a community access profile can enter the community. If a person wants to be notified when an entry is added to the community, that person must join the community and become a member. If an individual chooses not to join the community, they will still have access to allow for searching or browsing in the future.

Types of communications

There are two basic forms of communication that take place within a community of practice in the KN. A community discussion is a quick way to get a message out or ask a question to community members. This will not be validated or approved by the community manager, and is sent by e-mail directly to the community participants. Anybody who has access to the community has access to the community discussions.

The other type of communication that takes place is a 'knowledge entry', which is more formal and has a multi-part structure. The community manager must review and approve knowledge entries before they are sent to community members. While the manager must approve a knowledge entry before it becomes available to the community, either the author or the community manager can send it to other people for review or for comment prior to it being approved. Based on this review process, a knowledge entry can be edited at any time by the author or community manager. This process allows for validation and ensures confidence in the information contained in a knowledge entry.

Reference material on the KN

In addition to the communications that take place within a community, the KN allows for related reference material to be accessed from the community. In a section called Tools and Guides, the community manager can load or link to documents and files in many different formats that relate to the activity of the community. These documents and links can also be re-organised into folders by the community manager. The KN also includes a section called Standards and Specs, which allows the community manager to link to frequently used standards documents. These documents may be internal to Caterpillar or externally developed by a Standards Developing Organisation. There is no upload feature to the standards section, however, which ensures that community participants use only the controlled sources provided by our suppliers.

Value to the organisation

We have completed a study of the KN and found a return on the company's investment in excess of 200 per cent for internally focused communities, and over 700 per cent for externally focused communities. The primary benefits realised by users were improved productivity and quality. Studies have also shown that 67 per cent of the people looking for information found the results they needed using the KN. Furthermore, intangible benefits for Caterpillar include increased customer satisfaction with Caterpillar equipment, strengthened dealer and supplier relationships, increased retention of knowledge, improved collaboration skills, expansion of informal networks and continual learning.

As we go forward, we will invest more time and effort in the selection and training of the community managers. They play a key role in the vitality and success of each community. We are also looking at ways to provide additional support to strategic communities and leverage the benefits that the KN provides to the business as a whole. We have been amazed at the knowledge and expertise that has surfaced as a result of collaboration on the KN, often from some of the most unlikely places. The KN is truly changing the way we work at Caterpillar.

Reed Stuedemann is knowledge sharing manager at Caterpillar University. He can be contacted at stuedemann_reed_a@cat.com

10. Measuring and demonstrating the value of KM

Fulfilling the promise of KM at Fluor Corporation, a 2006 Global MAKE (Most Admired Knowledge Enterprise) winner. In this year's Global MAKE study, Fluor has been recognised for maximising the value of the company's enterprise intellectual capital. Fluor's Chairman, Alan Boeckmann, responded to the award by acknowledging that KM enables Fluor to leverage its global expertise and provide its clients with high-value solutions. **Rob E.V. Koene** *explains the part that KM measurement has played in Fluor's success.*

FLUOR CORPORATION is one of the world's largest, publicly-owned engineering, procurement, construction and maintenance (EPCM) services companies. The company is ranked in the top three of 'The Top Design-Build Firms' and 'The Top 400 Contractors' lists, which are compiled by Engineering News-Record (ENR) magazine. Employing nearly 35,000 employees worldwide, the company has worked on many of the world's most successful and demanding projects, and is widely regarded as one of the safest contractors.

Why KM at Fluor?

A project manager for a natural gas project in South Africa had a question about the next step in his project – he had some doubts about specifications given by the vendor on a piece of equipment and did not want to proceed without being sure. The issue was a showstopper. He didn't know the answer, and had to resolve the concern urgently in order to proceed with the project. Before he left the office for the day, he posted an urgent question to the knowledge community for help.

By the time he got to work the following morning, he had four replies from around the world. The responses confirmed that with a slight modification, his project could proceed.

This type of project problem solving occurs every day at Fluor. "This is not the first time I have had to resort to using the discussion forums to solve a problem," said the project manager. "I have found our knowledge-management (KM) tool and processes indispensable. When I first heard about KM, I had my doubts whether it would work. Today, I have my doubts whether I could work without it."

With projects all over the globe – many in remote locations – sharing knowledge on a global basis is essential to Fluor's success. In the face of increased international competition and to remain cost-competitive, the company has to perform increasing levels of work overseas in places such as New Delhi and Manila. The ability to share engineering services around the world helps the company to maintain around-the-clock effort and shorten time-to-market schedules. Fluor's KM strategy helps the company achieve business objectives by connecting people to people and solutions to challenges.

In 1999, to support Fluor's vision to be the premier provider of global, knowledge-based EPCM services, the company began its KM journey. The corporation recognised that its employees formed the core of its knowledge-based services, and that a better ability to link these employees in meaningful communities would not only allow them to access and share their collective knowledge, but would ultimately improve customer service. The company had been 'managing knowledge' for a long time, and pockets of the organisation were leveraging and sharing what they knew within their discipline in one office, but rarely on a global scale.

With employees as the core of Fluor's intellectual assets and knowledge-based services strategy, employee buy-in and participation are critical to the company's ability to grow. The ability to capture, share, leverage and improve what employees know in a global environment is a key differentiating factor. Fluor, like most organisations, is also faced with the challenges of an aging workforce, as well as a growing number of jobs being work-shared (supported by global offices) overseas. Both require ways to collect knowledge and share it before it walks out the door.

How did Fluor motivate employees while experiencing this flux in global employment? By communicating the benefit to employees – leverage knowledge, and make yourself more valuable to the corporation. A good colleague has always been someone that is ready to help and has a positive attitude.

A KM system just lets someone do that even better!

To help explain and teach the concepts of collaboration, Fluor adopted the following principles of knowledge sharing:

- Knowledge is an intangible asset;
- Knowledge management is 90 per cent connecting people, 10 per cent tool;
- We will actively encourage our members to collaborate;
- New knowledge is generated through sharing;
- Knowledge must be sustained through stewardship;
- Knowledge is shared across boundaries;
- Make the system accessible from any location (via the intranet or via secure internet links).

The benefits of KM at Fluor
- Enhance skill sets of all members;
- Leverage knowledge anytime, anyplace;
- Grow beyond internal capabilities;
- Provide optimal solutions for our customers;
- Improve overall business performance;
- Apply what we know to current and new markets;
- More effectively leverage our subject matter experts;
- Deliver value.

Where we are now
Employees in every office, business unit and discipline use the company's KM tool, Knowledge OnLine, as a resource to help them perform optimally. Effective KM derives the most from employees, intellectual property, suppliers, partners and customers. Having one enterprise solution puts employees on a common foundation for collaborative working and knowledge sharing, allowing the best ideas and people to shine.

However, the science of KM is still young in terms of practice, culture and supporting technology. At Fluor, we see new opportunities to continue to reduce the cost of KM and increase the value by making future investments in Knowledge OnLine.

The largest cost associated with a KM programme is the maintenance of existing content and development of new resources. On an ongoing basis, Fluor undertakes the elimination, integration and migration of old knowledge stores to Knowledge OnLine. The company believes that the context of knowledge (how, when and where to apply it) and association of experts is critical, but the actual content can often be supported and maintained by partners. For example, most Fluor projects involve equipment supplied by hundreds of different vendors. The vendors already have a large amount of knowledge about the equipment they manufacture, which is available on the internet. The tool should be able to easily combine and retrieve Fluor's expertise about how to properly design, engineer, construct and operate facilities, taking into account the knowledge maintained on the internet about the components that make up those facilities.

Another good example is the accessibility of all Quality Assurance (QA) documents, which enable staff to access the finer details of Fluor's work methods and QA.

Fluor's aim is to continue to raise the level of KM performance by encouraging knowledge innovation, work process improvement and strategic alignment of intellectual assets. The system will continue to evolve because new technologies will enable dynamic matching of the task context with solutions that more closely mimic how people interact with experts. This process will help accelerate and support the development of people into experts and better leverage their expertise.

Fluor's ability to access and share knowledge on a global, enterprise wide, real-time basis allows us to reap many benefits. Although the value is recognised internally and by our customers, it's clear there remains potential for even greater benefits. As time progresses, the company refines its KM strategy to align with current business goals. Success stories from all over the world and across business units are received daily and they continue to demonstrate the power of people connecting globally.

One of the success factors of Fluor's KM system is that it is people driven (not IT nor HR) and comes with an easy to use user interface. It includes a standard template for entering new knowledge and asking forum questions. The system also incorporates a powerful enterprise-search engine.

Creating value

Fluor's KM programme is valuable because it creates internal and external value, saving costs and resulting in better relationships with customers. In addition, the company places much emphasis on being a learning organisation. Knowledge OnLine is an effective system for training new hires, while people on job rotation can quickly find the education they need, when they need it. The benefits of a KM system, in this instance, far outweigh the costs.

Of course, the other value creating aspect is that created for Fluor's customers. While an elusive measurement since it relies totally on the feedback of engineers, this is the Holy Grail of any KM system. At Fluor, KM translates into huge cost savings with respect to early start-up (thus early production), lower project cost, fast resolution of problems, innovative solutions, etc.

Developing an effective KM programme requires real commitment to collaborative working practices. Today, there are 40 active communities with over 14,000 members in over 100 locations, conducting 3,500 searches each day, 500 downloads of knowledge objects daily, 250 new or updated knowledge objects each week, 150 questions and answers each week in the forums and 7,500 forum reads each week. The majority of these 'members' are engineers, designers and buyers. These are the people that create the value via their participation – asking questions, giving expert answers and submitting knowledge.

The trend is towards a culture where the amount of knowledge is increasing at a slower pace, while the number of forum questions is increasing. This phenomenon may be a sign of a maturing system where questions are asked about actual knowledge gaps or new developments. This is where Fluor's Global Experts play a major role in getting timely answers.

But there is no such thing as a free lunch. All KM systems come at a cost, and Fluor's consist of:

- Knowledge managers for the communities of practice;
- A small, centralised KM team focused on tool maintenance and development, community development and communications.

Internal value

In large part, the internal value is the money NOT spent by not having to invent the wheel several times and being able to connect members to experts worldwide. This value is derived, in part, from usage statistics, the digital footprints all users leave, for which Fluor has a robust tracking system.

These statistics are imported in a 'mathematical' model, a spreadsheet that links pre-determined categories of usage numbers to weighing factors, such as hours per unit. The resulting number is then multiplied by a unit cost. This is the gross saving, which is then deducted from the management costs involved. This results in a net total savings. In Fluor's case, these net savings exceed the cost by a factor of at least 20, which makes the system highly viable from an internal saving point of view.

Another factor that adds to the complexity and sometimes unexpected high (or low) numbers is the method of usage. Projects that are starting will have a hugely different usage pattern than projects in steady state or in their final stages. Fluor maintains a regular end-of-year review of the used weighing factors, making any necessary adjustments accordingly.

The main advantage of this approach is that a trend can easily be detected and that members can actually see a number, which is very powerful. The major disadvantage is that it cannot be presented in an attractive 'story' format, which most people relate well to.

As engineers, we love numbers, but they can also be a pitfall. The tendency is to crunch and slice and dice all available statistics. This is not wise. Select the BEHAVIOURS you want to measure and communicate and run the numbers on them. The old adage, 'What's measured gets done' applies. Make sure you are measuring and communicating the RIGHT BEHAVIOURS.

Customer value

The customer value is the value that the members create for Fluor's customers by finding smart solutions, getting round-the-clock advice from world-class experts and by being able to connect to the system from any location. This type of value is one of the most elusive to prove, but should prove the most exciting for any knowledge manager.

To put this into the context of a global engineering company such as Fluor: Engineers tend to regard the miracles they do as 'all in a regular work day' and thus not so special. The outside world tends to look at that a bit differently.

The challenge is to get engineers to tell the story without feeling like they are grandstanding or bragging about it. Having a KM system is just like owning and using a screwdriver – telling how you used it to bring an issue to a good end is something else.

Apart from Fluor, Shell EP has also been active in trying to capture 'success stories'. Shell claims a multi-million dollar saving on a worldwide basis. Fluor has an annual enterprise-wide success story and communications campaign called 'Knowvember'. Success stories are surfaced and judged by a panel of executives on their merit. The success story at the beginning of this article is a fine example of one of them.

Most of these customer-oriented success stories are usually expert solutions provided in a matter of days, enabling customers to solve engineering and design issues in a way that would be impossible to achieve without having a KM system. Communications by e-mail (one-to-few) would never have yielded the same results as the Knowledge OnLine forums (one-to-many).

Fluor assumes that by accumulating all resolved forums and the 24/7 access to experts and knowledge the company can demonstrate similar customer savings to those reported by Shell. Examples are fast start-ups, shorter project schedules, better informed decisions, etc.

One should remember that a refinery started up a few days ahead of schedule may represent a value of millions of dollars. From the context of submitted success stories, the 'expert' reader can fairly well estimate this customer saving.

One of the major difficulties in the surfacing of customer value may be the differences between cultures, with one more readily prepared to submit a success story than the other. This problem can be partly overcome by carefully targeting the cultural 'triggers' that every culture has. We have to remember that not all cultures have the same 'go-do' attitude.

Everyone working with colleagues or companies outside their own country or region has experienced this. A successful cultural targeting yields huge returns in view of submitted success stories and their contents.

Resources
SiteScape's case study of Shell EP:
http://www.sitescape.com/site/content/clients_partners/pdfs/shell.pdf

Rob E.V. Koene is Global Knowledge Manager, Engineering, Electrical & Control Systems Community, Fluor Corp. He can be contacted at rob.koene@fluor.com

11. Applying KM to improve quality

Sanjay Swarup *explains how best-practice replication at Ford enhances quality-improvement practices and encourages collaborative working.*

USE OF 6-Sigma and other quality-improvement programmes is very prevalent. What is rare is a robust business process to replicate quality-improvement practices across all business units of an enterprise. To tackle this challenge, what is needed is a proven process to capture, share, and fully leverage any and all quality improvements that occur in remote corners of an enterprise.

Using specific actual cases and related metrics, this article shows how Ford Motor Company, since 1995, has successfully used a web-based KM enabler, called best-practice replication, or BPR, to replicate and leverage quality improvement practices across the enterprise.

In 2001, Dearborn Assembly Plant, in Dearborn, near Detroit, MI, was producing 100,000 units/year of the popular Mustang sports car. Some isolated reports indicated that the air-conditioners were not cool enough.

Gilbert Johnston, automation engineer, and John Kraatz, product specialist, both at Dearborn Assembly Plant, led the investigation, which revealed that the air-conditioners were performing to specifications, but the problem was, in some cases, that the air was not consistently cool. Investing in new technology of small thermal sensors coupled with low-cost, hand-held, infra-red temperature scanners and using a range of acceptable temperatures, Johnston and Kraatz were able to pinpoint the problem to defective airflow. Knowing this, corrective actions were taken. The improved air-flow eliminated the inconsistent temperatures. This resulted in a 75 per-cent increase in customer satisfaction and cost savings due to reduced warranty claims.

On 7 March 2001, Gilbert entered this proven practice (#928 in the 'Vehicle Operations Final Assembly' Community of Practice) into best-practice replication. BPR is Ford Motor Company's intranet-based application that enables manufacturing and non-manufacturing communities of practice, with worldwide locations, to capture, share and replicate best practices.

Using BPR, this quality improvement was then replicated at ten other Vehicle Assembly Plants, including Kansas City Assembly Plant, Kentucky Assembly Plant, Oakville (Canada) Assembly Plant, Michigan Truck Plant, near Detroit, MI, Norfolk Assembly Plant, and Twin Cities Assembly Plant.

Maumee Stamping Plant, Maumee, OH, a suburb of Toledo, OH, produces 115,000 tons of steel and 300 tons of aluminium fenders for the popular Ford Explorer, Ford 150 pick-up and many other Ford vehicles annually. Stamped parts are typically put on an inspection conveyor line that moves at the rate of 16 parts per minute. Inspectors stationed along the conveyor have less than four seconds a stamping to check for splits, tears and depressions in the stamping. Typically, these defects are caused by the inferior quality of incoming material. By the time an inspector is able to identify a defective fender and stop the line, about eight to ten defective parts have already streamed by. This involves stopping the line, having a 'material handler' retrieve the defective fenders, tag each fender, and then stack them at the parts re-claim area. (On a periodic basis, the salvageable defective fenders are repaired and re-inspected – a costly process.) Then the conveyor line is re-started. Clearly this process was leading to high repair costs and reducing productivity.

Gale Doremus, quality co-ordinator at Maumee Stamping Plant, and her team investigated ways to correct the situation. They came up with a quadrant-inspection method. This involved visually dividing each stamping into four quadrants. Inspectors were now requested to inspect only the top-right quadrant of the first stamping, then only the bottom-right quadrant of the next stamping, then only the bottom-left quadrant of the next stamping, and finally only the top-left quadrant of the next stamping. They would then resume inspecting only the top-right quadrant of the next stamping, thus repeating the cycle.

Using this quadrant-inspection process dramatically reduced the number of defective fenders. Now when an inspector identifies a defective fender and stops the line, only about two to three defective parts have streamed by. This not only reduced the number of defective parts, but also reduced the manpower assigned for re-claiming and re-inspecting. It also improved customer satisfaction with higher-quality fenders.

On 27 July 2001, this proven practice (#10 in the 'Stamping' Community of Practice) was entered into BPR by Gale Doremus.

Using BPR, this quality improvement was then replicated at seven other plants including Buffalo Stamping Plant, Flat Rock (MI) Stamping Plant, Dearborn (MI) Stamping Plant, Hermosillo (MX) Stamping Plant, and Woodhaven (OH) Stamping Plant.

In 2003, the Ford Motor Credit Company's Colorado Springs Service Center had six Access databases and three Excel spreadsheets to track skip accounts. A skip account is a delinquent account for which reasonable efforts to determine the location of the customer and vehicle have been unsuccessful. Characteristics of a skip account may include the following: disconnected or invalid phone numbers; unemployed/ unable to verify employment; returned mail with no forwarding address; information from other creditors indicating a possible skip.

To find a way to streamline this process a 6-Sigma project was executed by Black Belt Mike Delmonico.

As a result of this 6-Sigma project, Delmonico was able to identify a way to consolidate these multiple sources of information into one skip database. By establishing a common database, the team was able to establish consistency in reporting and comparing 'skip' accounts across service centres. This enabled them to enhance productivity and reduce costs.

On 29 July 2003, this proven practice (#7, in the Ford Financial-Global Operations & Technology) was entered into BPR by the local BPR Focal Point.

Using BPR, these quality improvements, productivity enhancements and cost-reduction steps were leveraged across the enterprise, when this practice was replicated at all nine regional offices.

These are just three examples of more than 10,200 proven process-improvement practices that have been captured and replicated using Ford Motor Company's Best Practice Replication since 1995. A significant number of these practices are related to improving quality. Each one of these practices has been replicated by an average of at least six or more sites.

This process of replication has helped leverage the quality improvements identified by the originators of the proven practices to percolate and permeate across the many service centres and 108 plants in 26 countries that make up the sprawling enterprise of Ford Motor Company.

Quality improvement is taken seriously

Many of the readers of this article have surely heard the Ford tag line, 'Quality is Job 1'. This is not just a tag line, but an overall corporate policy at Ford. Supporting this policy are three key top-down strategies:

1. Quality Operating System (QOS): Launched in the 1990s, this ensures adherence to a common standard set for procedures, guidelines, standards and metrics that are 'critical to quality';
2. Quality Leadership Initiative (QLI): Established in 2002 to support the company's back-to-basics strategy. The purpose of the QLI is to engage all employees to improve quality and customer satisfaction jointly as a team;
3. Consumer Driven 6-Sigma: Launched in 1999 to improve quality faster. 6-Sigma is a methodology that applies a set of statistical tools to reduce and eliminate defects, and also help improve quality of products and services.

Supporting these three top-down systems is a bottom-up employee-based KM system, including best-practice replication, which allows employees to capture and share proven quality improvement practices.

What are the results of these efforts?

It is truly gratifying to note the results of replication on on-going quality improvements, as reported by newspapers and trade publications:

- "Between 1998 and 2003, Ford has improved about 18 per cent in initial quality", Brian Walters, director of Quality Research at JD Power Associates, in 'Ford's Quality Battle, Serious efforts appear to be paying off', Automotive Industries, June 2003;
- "Ford Motor Company reduced warranty costs by about $1bn since 2001", as quoted by the VP of quality, Detroit Free Press, 8 December 2004;
- "Since 6-Sigma's inception (1999), Ford has saved about $1bn in waste elimination globally. Year-over-year savings worldwide were $359m last year". 6 Sigma in 'Ford Revisited', Quality Digest, June 2003.

Of course, the company's BPR system cannot take credit for all of the above results; however, it certainly can take credit for a significant portion of the improvements.

Why use KM to leverage quality efforts?

With a robust and active KM programme, quality efforts can be leveraged from a local level to an enterprise level. Also, KM can be used to maximise value generated at the local level to the enterprise level. Finally, a KM programme can leverage a local quality improvement effort to the enterprise level.

Getting maximum value of quality-improvement efforts

Since 1996, BPR has been averaging close to 10,000 replications per year. There are currently 53 active communities of practice, each one supported by a Gatekeeper and an average of 50 Focal Points. This, coupled with a high level of enterprise-wide quality-improvement efforts, has helped Ford Motor Company generate a value of $1.25 billion. This goes to show that high rewards that can be generated when a high level of KM activity is combined with a high level of quality-improvement activity.

What have we learnt about how to apply KM to improve quality?

Here are some of the lessons that we have learnt. The KM system should have pre-defined metrics to measure the value of the captured knowledge. Defining metrics to capture the value of the practice is vital information for the replicating location. As an example, BPR has a total of 168 different types of value metrics. Each of these value metrics can be classified into six broad categories:

- Safety: Injury lost time rate as measured by events/200k hours, Injury Severity Rate as measured by % decrease, Ergonomics as measured by Rx case, etc.
- Cost: Annual Savings in $/year, Cycle Time Savings as measured by Minutes/Unit, Energy Usage as measured in $/year, etc.
- Motivation: Absenteeism, as measured by % decrease in absenteeism; Medical Costs as measured by $/year, etc.
- Environment: Packaging costs as measured by $/year; Waste Minimisation as measured by costs $/year, etc.
- Delivery: First Time Through as measured in $/year; Total Dock-to-Dock Time as measured in $/year, etc;
- Quality: Defects as measured by defects/million; Customer Satisfaction as measure by percentage improvement; Error Rate as measured by percentage decrease, etc.

These metrics are built into the BPR KM system. Every time a practice is captured, the BPR system prompts the user to identify the value/benefits derived from adopting the practice.

1. The KM system should enable enterprise-wide capture of quality-improvement practices. The value of any quality improvement can be greatly magnified if the KM system is designed to capture any and all quality enhancements from all units of the enterprise.

    The infra-red temperature scanner example was captured by a vehicle assembly plant in Dearborn, MI, the quadrant inspection example was captured by the stamping plant in Maumee, OH, and the skip-tracing report example was captured by a Ford Credit office, in Colorado. Each of these practices was not only captured by different locations, but also by different divisions. Also, in each of these cases, the benefits accrued to the originating plant were leveraged multifold by having a KM system that enabled the enterprise-wide replication of the proven practices.

2. The KM system should be designed to enable capture of 6-Sigma replicable findings. At Ford, a Black Belt cannot close a 6-Sigma project unless the Black Belt responds to a prompt for identifying any replicable findings. If the response is in the affirmative, the Black Belt is encouraged to contact the local BPR Focal Point to enter the replicable findings into the BPR system. When the local BPR Focal Point enters the replicable findings into BPR, and this is approved by the appropriate community Gatekeeper, the replicable findings can be replicated by other sites.

    The 6-Sigma Black Belt project to consolidate multiple repositories of skip-trace reporting was replicated at nine facilities because the BPR system had to have the ability to capture the replicable finding of the 6-Sigma project.

3. The KM system should capture metrics on replication efforts of proven quality-improvement practices.

    In today's hyperactive economy, everybody is busy. Given this scenario, people will only replicate practices that have defined value metrics.

    The infra-red temperature scanner practice had value in quality improvements. The quadrant inspection practice had value in cost savings, as well as quality improvement. The skip-tracing practice had value in improved productivity, reduced costs, as well providing a communised reporting system.

4. Leadership must provide ongoing encouragement, recognition and support for the capturing and replication of quality-improvement practices.

    In BPR typically the leadership provides peer recognition during staff meetings to all employees responsible for entering proven practices into BPR as well to those who replicated proven practices submitted by others.

    Recognition certificates are provided to the originators of a best practice, as well as to those who replicate best practices.

Conclusion

The price of entry in today's brutal marketplace is the delivery of high-quality products and services. In order to meet this challenge, 6-Sigma and other quality improvement programmes can provide added benefit by using replication processes such as BPR. Citing specific examples, this article shows that coupled with quality improvement programmes, a robust KM system enables an enterprise to capture, share and replicate quality improvement practices throughout the organisation.

Ford Motor Company

Ford Motor Company designs, manufactures, markets and finances automotive vehicles in 200 markets across six Continents. Ford is ranked # 4 by Fortune 500 and had $171 billion in global revenues in 2004. Ford has 324,000 employees globally and celebrated its 100 anniversary in 2003. For company information visit www.ford.com.

Many Ford Motor Company staff members, including Gale Doremus, Mike Delmonico, Gilbert Johnston, John Kraatz and Linda Carter, contributed to this chapter.

Sanjay Swarup is senior knowledge management specialist at Ford Motor Company. He can be contacted at sswarup@ford.com

12. Halliburton: A sustained commitment to collaboration

Jerry Ash describes how Halliburton's KM programme, founded on communities of practice, ensures its long-term sustainability by building tangible, bottom-line value.

Here's how you ensure the sustainability of your KM programme: make sure you have the support of management at launch; connect to the issues that keep executives awake at night, but don't pick battles you can't win; be 100 percent successful and prove it; and, make sure no-one overlooks the real value added.

It's not quite as simple as that, but those are the keystones of a four-year-old KM initiative at Houston-based Halliburton that has given life to a strategy and a hypothesis for sustainability (see sidebar 'Halliburton's KM hypothesis' on page 74) that are one and the same. There is nothing intangible about knowledge work at Halliburton and there is no mistaking its value – ever.

The Halliburton hypothesis doesn't pretend to be a complete formula for success, but experience over four years suggests that failure to follow any one of these guidelines will lead to trouble. Perhaps it's time to stop calling it a hypothesis.

In the experience of Michael Behounek, director of KM at the company, a KM project that starts by shortening this list faces the likelihood it will fail. In one particular case, one of the technology groups began following only part of the hypothesis and its KM project did not work. The team was forced to go back to the KM core team to facilitate a relaunch.

The history

The strategy and sustainability hypothesis began in mid-2001 based on the vision and drive of one of the company's senior executives. Halliburton has two major operating groups: the Energy Services Group (ESG) with 35,000 employees, and KBR (which stands for Kellogg-Brown-Root) with 65,000 employees. The company had a trio of CEOs, one company-wide and one for each of the two groups (see sidebar 'About KM and Halliburton' on page 73).

The company's overall vision, and ESG CEO Edgar Ortiz's personal vision, is to be "the real-time knowledge company serving the upstream petroleum industry". The ESG had already spent many years connecting and building an infrastructure to electronically move, store and analyse data. The next step was to leverage this infrastructure by connecting the explicit information it contained with 35,000 employees in over 100 countries. But there was one problem: although there had already been notable successes on the technical side of KM, too many people saw its front-line use as a very fuzzy concept. Worse, there were few case studies that demonstrated KM's clear business value or a pragmatic strategy and methodology for KM implementation.

A scoping team was therefore asked to study the issues and return to the senior-management team with a recommendation on how to take KM forwards. Michael Behounek was part of that team. "We immediately recognised we were late to the game," he says. "The best thing we could do was learn quickly what was or was not working in other companies."

The team contacted the American Productivity and Quality Center (APQC) – also based in Houston – and solicited the help of APQC president Carla O'Dell to investigate and help synthesise what was working. The team examined more than 15 different companies, their approaches, systems, methodologies and results.

From this investigation, the hypothesis on what would work began to form and the team proposed three pilots to test the concepts in several parts of the business. The initiatives needed to be pragmatic, systematic and able to deliver measurable business results. They also had to solve large and complex business issues.

In time, Behounek became director of a new KM core team composed of five veterans with a total of 118 years of operations, management and KM experience among them.

The approach

The components of the initial KM pilots were drawn from bits and pieces of KM programmes at several other companies. "We tried to assemble them all into a coherent, systematic approach that delivered real business value," Behounek says.

Since these early stages, all of the KM initiatives at the organisation have been project-based and built around communities of practice. To date, the core team has assisted the formation of 19 communities and all have proven successful. Each had a unique business case and each exceeded its original target, as verified by the relevant business unit. The communities are by no means static. They are organic in nature and evolve and adapt to new business needs. Some communities have split, others have merged.

Halliburton communities use most of the common KM tools and find big benefits in quality tools, social-network analysis and surveys. IT is used as the enabler for knowledge creation. Each of the 19 communities has from one to five full-time 'knowledge brokers' to moderate, facilitate discussion threads and steward the repositories. The brokers are not experts. Their subject-matter understanding is broad, but not deep. As users enter questions and issues, people respond to the various threads. The brokers engage subject-matter experts to validate the best global answer or provide one that had not been documented before. Therefore, knowledge is verified and the process is transparent, which in turn increases trust. Only three of the 19 communities are restricted due to intellectual-property issues. The KM core team prefers to leave communities open unless there are significant business reasons not to.

Communities span many different areas inside the company, from support of service quality in product service lines to technology innovation, functional support groups and even the enterprise-resource-planning system. Users are equally diverse – from PhDs to field personnel based in warehouses, factories, central office or remote parts of the world.

The value proposition

Obtaining and maintaining management sponsorship in the executive suite or the business unit depends on tying KM projects and P&L responsibilities together. As Behounek says, "VPs feel they need to deliver. In the long run, if managers feel KM is not delivering, they will begin questioning expenditures, time and effort – usually at budget time."

Halliburton views each community as an investment and expects each to be 100 per cent successful in delivering a substantiated return on investment. That's why the core team insists each community needs a balanced scorecard and auditable financial method to determine ongoing performance and ultimate value. The process used is based on 6-Sigma and performance-improvement methods. "Of course," Behounek concedes, "KM cannot be quantified fully by monetary values, and so we use a balanced-scorecard approach. Since in many cases it is not possible to establish direct cause and effect relationships, it is worth using multiple measures in areas where KM should be having an impact. If these measures all point in the same direction, then you can state the systematic effect produced by KM. If the scorecard shows no results, then the decision needs to be made whether to stop the effort or change the scope of the project."

"Nearly all the KM programmes I have examined at other companies have not been diligent in actually getting the detailed numbers in a systematic fashion," Behounek continues. "Instead, the financial value is inferred." It is Behounek's opinion that a failure to provide hard numbers causes a risk to the sustainability of the broader KM programme, particularly during a downturn or when new management moves into place. "If you fail to provide real proof, these numbers are at worst dismissed or at best viewed very sceptically by management," he says.

Behounek outlines the litmus test he employs: "If you are truly adding financial value on the scale I see quoted by many KM programmes, then you should show evidence on the company's annual report. I therefore have a close relationship with our accountant. Six Sigma principles stress the importance of this over and over."

At the same time, it is easier to establish hard figures for KM programmes that are tied directly to the business process. All 19 projects at Halliburton were selected based on the ability of KM to have a measurable impact on the bottom line. Imagine, for example, the effect of an annual ROI figure of 564 per cent on management thinking. Halliburton's 'Employee Central' portal was built to encourage 30,000 of its employees to work together to solve problems from field locations, client sites and offices around the world. The portal captures information from SAP's financial and human-resource systems, Interwoven document and content-management applications, and several technical oil and gas systems used to manage the company's various drilling and surveying businesses. Through collaboration and problem solving between employees in Halliburton outposts around the world, faster response time and increased service quality have produced an estimated $20 million of benefits per year. The following sections outline two more cases in point.

Case history: SAP procurement and material community

As a large, diverse company operating around the globe, Halliburton recognised there was a significant opportunity for cost savings through improvement in its procurement and inventory-management processes. While the implementation of SAP provided many benefits to the company, the system also added a degree of complexity for the individuals responsible for procurement and inventory management, leading to high purchasing, inventory and logistics costs, inaccurate inventories, and long lead times.

A team was chartered to work with Halliburton's KM team to investigate the problems and develop a solution. The first step was a root-cause analysis and a review of company-audit reports. This analysis made clear that training and transfer of good practices and lessons learnt was critical for solving the problems incurred. For several weeks, the team worked to design the processes and tools needed by a community of practice to give all of the people involved in procurement and materials the ability to connect to each other, to experts and to necessary content.

Deployment of SAP had been a long and expensive process, but deployment of a global community took less than 30 days, using a network of 'local champions' and virtual training sessions. The community now has four knowledge brokers in various parts of the world who facilitate virtual discussions, connect members with experts as necessary, and capture good practices and lessons learnt so that they can be shared. This means that the procurement specialist in Egypt can post a question to the community at 10am her time and be assured a response before anyone even arrives for work at the Houston office.

The community has been active since the initial roll-out, currently averaging well over 500 unique users accessing the collaboration tool approximately 3,000 times per month. During 2003, there were a total 37,815 log-ons in the P&M Portal. Just half way through 2004, there were 31,859. In a recent survey, completed by 235 community members, 73 per cent reported measurable time savings from participating in the community.

But, though impressive, these are the kinds of soft numbers KM initiatives too often rely on. The true measure of success is the business result. During the first year the community was in place, the company recognised a $71.5 million cost saving in procurement and materials. While KM was not the only factor in that improvement, senior leaders agree that it was an important contributing factor.

Examples of smaller business gains could be directly attributed to KM, including:

- Reduced 'request for service' tickets per month. Now that the community answers many of these questions, the experts in the help centre say they are saving at least ten hours a month, worth $1,000;
- The community has acted as a source of training and has also provided mentoring, which has led to a reduction in the cost of unreconciled inventory in Saudi Arabia from $700k to $250k;
- A single instance of collaborative working saved over $10,000 in one shipping event in the Middle East.

Case history: Electronic technician community

The high-pressure pumping and mixing process for fracturing, acidising and cementing has become more automated during the past ten years. This automation allows for consistency, but has also added new operational and maintenance processes. Just three years ago, Halliburton ESG noted that electronic technicians were required on 80 per cent of fracturing jobs to ensure that the electronics performed flawlessly. Technicians were difficult resources to hire and train to meet the demand of customers at each well site.

Halliburton's KM group facilitated the creation of a small team of electronic technicians for a three-month period in late 2001 to help understand the business needs and design a solution that would improve pumping job-service quality, reduce non-productive time and decrease the need for electronic technicians to intervene at individual well sites.

Together, the electronic technicians and KM group were able to design a KM solution. Essentially, electronic technicians needed to be connected to experts and to each other so that the experience of the entire group could be used to troubleshoot and solve problems, rather than relying on the limited knowledge of one individual isolated at a customer's well site. The group therefore developed a collaborative, problem-solving community to provide 24/7 peer-to-peer training, troubleshooting and support.

The team defined the community and processes required for the technicians to discuss issues and share good practices. The group developed an easy-to-use portal interface, which was designed around a collaboration tool that allows the community to share its knowledge and get answers to questions. The interface also provides access to vital documents and contact information for leading experts on various pieces of hardware to ensure immediate answers to urgent technical questions. The community was launched in December 2001 and today is a thriving knowledge-sharing network of more than 200 users in numerous locations around the world. Interestingly, the number of users is greater than the actual number of electronic technicians within the community.

In 2003, individual instances of knowledge sharing generated, in one way or another, over $1.4 million for Halliburton. In addition, electronic technicians report time savings of approximately 20 per cent due to the community. This has allowed the company to meet the demands of business growth without employing additional technicians. The technicians it currently has are also better trained and more effective than ever. They have reduced the number of repeat repairs, measured through SAP work orders, from 30 per cent to virtually zero.

> **About KM and Halliburton**
> Halliburton is structured around two operating units worldwide: the Energy Services Group (ESG), which provides upstream petroleum services and consulting to clients such as Shell, BP, ExxonMobil, Total, Petrobras etc; and, KBR, which provides support ranging from government and services infrastructure to refineries, liquid natural gas and fertiliser plants. KBR's government-services division is the operation most often in the news, the division regarded by the popular press as 'Halliburton'.
>
> But regardless of KBR's high profile and larger work force, it is ESG's divisions that account for the majority of the Halliburton's profit. ESG was for a long time also the location of Behounek's KM team, which focuses on a subset of employees who are PC-based (roughly 15,000 employees). The KM programme reaches over 8,000 unique users. This year, the KM core team has launched a major programme to reach field employees who cannot connect easily to the network (roughly another 20,000 people). The KM team will be offering access via any internet connection.

Relationship to hierarchy

During the developmental years of KM, there was a general belief that the open, cross-functional, intangible nature of KM could not be directly tied to the business goals and objectives of an organisation, and therefore the ROI could not be quantified. Not so at Halliburton. The KM initiative was initiated at the highest corporate level and the KM core team was located close to the hierarchy from the beginning, focusing

> **Halliburton's KM hypothesis**
> To assure a sustainable KM programme, an organisation needs to create sustainable KM, by providing:
>
> - Executive sponsorship;
>   - At the business-unit level;
>   - For a small core team.
> - A focus on a vital business need and an articulated business case;
>   - Don't be a company-wide initiative;
>   - Be project based.
> - Budget for appropriate resources, including time and funds;
>   - Ensure sustainability, by providing a KM process design that includes
>   - Dedicated facilitation, embedded leadership
>   - Easy-to-use tools
>   - Integration into users' workflow;
>   - Reciprocity;
>
> Help sustainability, by:
>
> - Focusing on solutions that assist the organisation in problem solving;
>   - At the business-unit level, to drive productivity, quality and innovation;
>   - At the job-role level, to help people in their daily work life (reciprocity).
> - Collaboration, which is key and requires focus on the organisational environment;
> - Targeting a business need; don't be a hammer looking for a nail;
> - Tying into existing efforts and initiatives;
> - Paying attention to details; shortcuts are dangerous.
>
> To maintain sustainability, KM programmes must be able to:
>
> - Provide intrinsic rewards by making people more effective;
> - Provide validated, trusted information and solutions;
> - Adapt to meet changing business needs over time;
> - Prove value with a continuous measurement system.
>   - Financial;
>   - Business objectives;
>   - Input, process, output.
>
> Each item is a must and requires constant attention. The hypothesis surmises that failure in any one category can lead to failure of the whole project.

directly on specific operational functions and projects.

In December 2004, a change in the organisational structure further clarified the core team's status as an integral part of the business. A new COO position was created and the organisational chart divided the company into three major units: the two major businesses (ESG and KBR) and Functions. The Functions unit includes Supply Chain and Management Systems (SC&MS), IT, Marketing and Strategy, ESG HR, KBR HR, Security, and Aviation. The concept of SC&MS is similar to the principles made famous by the likes of Wal-Mart and Dell. The strategy is to bring more value to the bottom line by focusing on procurement and materials functions, manufacturing, logistics and so on.

The KM core team resides with SC&MS, which reports to the COO. The Management Systems component represents the company-wide processes, standards and guidelines that all businesses need, including such functions as quality systems, safety systems and now KM. Knowledge management is viewed as an overall management process that helps operational units create, distribute, share and use knowledge throughout the company. The new structure makes it possible for the KM core team to assist both ESG and KBR. It is envisioned that the KM core team will extend its reach from ESG to the entire company by the end of this year.

The 19 communities of practice facilitated so far by the Halliburton KM core team have generated numerous instances of success. These are supported by hard numbers and reinforced by a KM quarterly report that keeps the attention of management on the ever-expanding and solid business case for KM. The knowledge factor is gaining attention as the core team functions as an integral part of Supply Chain and Management Systems group and extends its reach under the new COO to include both ESG and KBR business units.

For more information and the complete text of a STAR Series Dialogue with Michael Behounek at the Association of Knowledgework, go to www.kwork.org/Stars/stars.html#2004

Jerry Ash is US correspondent for Inside Knowledge. He can be contacted at jash@kwork.org

13. Answering the question

Simon Walker *explains how a knowledge sharing system that puts the right answers in front of technical support staff throughout its European operations helps to give Lucent Technologies a key competitive edge.*

UNTIL THE mid-1990s, the telecoms equipment market was almost as sleepy as its customers – growing at a regular single-digit percentage almost every year. That is not to say that it was not competitive, but since the rise in popularity of the internet, the pace of change has speeded up dramatically and the market has become positively cut-throat. Even the smallest mis-steps in business strategy or pricing can be fatal – as Marconi found out last year, for example.

Lucent Technologies is one of the longest-established communications equipment suppliers in the world. It designs and delivers the systems, services and software to support both current telecoms networks, as well as the 'next generation' converged voice and data networks that the world's major network operators, such as BT, are already building.

For companies such as Lucent, the diversity of communications choices that operators and consumers enjoy only adds to the complexity. Lucent needs to combine its strengths in mobile, optical, software, data and voice networking technologies, as well as services, to create new revenue-generating opportunities for its customers, while enabling them to quickly deploy and better manage their networks.

This complex and competitive environment therefore generates substantial pressure on the productivity of the support analysts, the people who support customers and engineers in the field and who often need to come up with solutions to problems in double-quick time.

In this article I will introduce Lucent's knowledge-sharing system, which was recently implemented in the services division, and the deployment of the 'Ask Lucent' programme in the customer-support division covering 11 countries and 400 staff in Europe.

The idea? To leverage the value of the collective knowledge of its services community to deliver more effective and higher quality services to customers.

Support organisations face enormous challenges in the telecoms market due to the growth, complexity and diversity of the products. Unlike, for example, consumer PC support, vendors cannot put just anyone on the front-line – support staff must have an in-depth understanding of the products and customers' common problems and customers cannot be left waiting for an answer.

The answer, we felt, was to build a new system that places a premium not just on the effective generation, but also the re-use, of knowledge.

Ask Lucent

Lucent therefore devised a 'knowledge-centred support' strategy based on a knowledgebase developed in the US called Ask Lucent. The idea of Ask Lucent was to leverage the thousands of customer transactions that service staff handle every year in order to develop a self-service facility for customers and employees.

Initially, the knowledgebase would be pre-populated with the answers to common questions about products that support is most frequently asked. When the knowledgebase lacks the answers to a question, support staff – when they find an answer that works for the customer – can add an entry and share their knowledge with everyone else in the support organisation across Europe.

The idea of the strategy is to propel information outward, as close to the customer as possible. If relevant and well-crafted answers to questions are available, customers are normally happy to serve themselves, and analysts at Lucent are able to find solutions to support problems faster and more effectively.

Working with the knowledge base, junior analysts learn faster, require less training time and can respond to a broader range of issues by applying known solutions. The ultimate outcome is that customers can find answers and solve their own problems, reducing support calls entirely and empowering them with immediate, 'on demand' support.

Entries are therefore not just thrown into Ask Lucent. When an analyst creates a solution, it is reviewed by technical experts to ensure that the quality and integrity of the knowledgebase is maintained. The teams are a virtual global community, all with specialist understanding of particular products, who work to ensure the accuracy and consistency of Ask Lucent.

But knowledge-centred support requires a new process where knowledge is the most important asset when analysts work through the problem resolution process. In Lucent, we developed a knowledge-centric support process that would be integral to the success of the deployment methodology.

Business objectives
To maintain our focus during the implementation process, the following guiding objectives were devised. We needed to:

- Increase operational efficiency – reduce re-work, the number of escalations and the time to resolve 'assistance requests' raised by customers;
- Improve customer satisfaction;
- Help increase profitability – having assistance request dealt with by ordinary engineers, enabling our most best engineers to focus on high value activities;
- Cultivate a knowledge-sharing culture that would help drive innovation in Lucent.

The specific outcomes were expected to be:

- Improved quality of solutions to customers;
- Consistent provision of solutions;
- Increasing first-call resolution;
- Reduced costs per call;
- Fewer calls to the support desk;
- Accelerated training;
- Increasing employee satisfaction.

To achieve these outcomes the knowledge-centric support process needed to be embedded into the organisation.

Deployment framework
The deployment framework followed a participatory action research (PAR) methodology. PAR is a process that involves inquiry in which researchers and the 'researched' form collaborative relations in order to identify and address mutually conceived issues – or problems – through cycles of action and research. The cycle includes the 'plan', 'act', 'observe' and 'reflect' stages:

- **Plan.** Involves developing an understanding of what is required to deploy the programme successfully in the first phase;
- **Act.** The implementation of the plan;
- **Observe.** Proactive monitoring of the success of the activity incorporating the collection of information to help determine what was good and bad with the deployment;
- **Reflect.** After each phase we reflected on the deployment to work out what worked well and what the barriers were. This is incorporated into the planning of next phase – learn from doing.

The initial focus of that research was to generate a deeper understanding of the barriers to deploying KM, an understanding that would help us to avoid the common pitfalls and enable us to build the foundations for greater success for KM projects in the future.

A key component of the PAR framework was the recruitment of 'champions' for each country to lead and deploy the programme in their respective teams. We believed their involvement would be critical in overcoming national and organisational culture barriers – as the system was to be rolled out to more than 400 staff across 11 countries in Europe – as well as helping to overcome natural opposition to change.

Communication between the project teams and the champions was two-way. That is to say, the champions regularly updated the team so that they could incorporate the particular needs of such communities in planning and roll-out.

Our approach was to deploy the programme piece-by-piece geographically, while simultaneously reflecting on practice to understand the challenges we faced and what action was required to overcome the barriers at each stage. The deployment was structured as a three-phase project:

- **Cycle one** – pilot: United Kingdom (June 2004 – October 2004);
- **Cycle two**: Belgium, Netherlands, Poland, Czech Republic, Ireland and Germany (November 2004 – September 2005);
- **Cycle three:** Spain, Russia, Italy, Portugal and France (October 2005 – December 2005).

The first phase was a pilot in the UK so that we could start by developing a solid understanding of what was required to be successful, including the development of project documentation.

We started with the premise that the Ask Lucent initiative could be deployed as a project. But we soon realised that moulding a KM initiative of any magnitude into a highly disciplined and tangible framework would not be easy. Can you deploy a KM initiative by segmenting it into discrete work packages incorporating detailed executable tasks?

As we began the pilot in the UK we realised that there was far more to this programme than telling the end-users, 'there's the technology, away you go'. Engaging the hearts and minds of the support community would be about more than technology. We started to realise that their focus was on metrics – how quickly a customer enquiry can be dealt with, how many times clients have to come back with the same query, and so on.

It was therefore difficult to move from a metrics-oriented mindset to a knowledge-centric culture and we quickly found that this initiative would be more about cultural change than simply performing tasks on a new technology platform.

The cultural element also highlights the following question that we needed to answer: do you select KM strategies that are congruent with the existing organisational culture or try to change the culture to fit with the strategy? As support organisations generally work in geographical and business unit silos we believed the culture would need to change for the Ask Lucent strategy to be successful.

This would require greater collaboration across business silos; building a greater understanding of cultural nuances and adapting the KM programme to meet the particular needs of each community – something that will take time.

We continued to develop a project definition report and evolve our understanding of what was required to be successful. We deployed the programme with what we knew and started to see success with customers serving themselves, and support analysts creating high quality content and re-using content to help solve repeat problems.

As with all initiatives we had the early adopters – those who took to the new system enthusiastically – and those who required a little more persuasion. From our early experience we developed a number of attributes that seemed to indicate a likelihood of success:

- Sustained senior leadership buy-in;
- Technology that is easy to use and seamlessly integrated into existing platforms;
- A high level of trust, so that staff feel that knowledge sharing will increase their job security, not undermine it;
- A focus on value-creating objectives rather than dry operational metrics – focus on positive trends, not numbers;
- Integration of a KM recognition programme into the existing human resources performance management frameworks;
- A good answer to the key question, 'what's in it for me?';
- A strong correlation between Ask Lucent's performance and a clear indication of how it helped Lucent achieve its strategic goals;
- A job specification for the country-champion role to ensure we recruit staff with the appropriate knowledge, skills and abilities;
- A clear definition of what success will look like;
- An effective communication package aimed at all key stakeholders about programme deployment and operational status.

After phase one – the pilot test in the UK – we conducted an after-action review to capture our key learnings and to ensure that we were all 'on the same page' with what we were trying to achieve. The review included the following four steps:

- What was supposed to happen?
- What actually happened?
- Why was there a difference?
- What can we learn from this?

We would have all the key ingredients that would provide us with a recipe for success in phases two and three. We knew, however, that a large percentage of KM initiatives fail to deliver on expectation, so we created a 'risk register' to capture key barriers that we might encounter, which we continuously updated and managed throughout the deployment.

The next phase

As per everything we had learnt in phase one, we started by recruiting and training the champions for phase two and provided the management community with various presentations to ensure that they would be fully supportive of everything required to deploy the programme successfully in their region. This, of course, stressed the benefits to them in clear business terms.

This caused some upheaval. Staff were required to follow a new knowledge problem-solving process. In other words, the way they had worked for the last decade was changing. This was a challenge for some of our longer-serving support analysts.

The champions helped update our generic project plan regularly to include the cultural and business requirements of their teams to ensure that our plan encompassed the cultural heterogeneity of the various countries of Europe. As we began to execute on the plans we began to understand why driving corporate change of any kind is never straightforward – no matter how rigorous the planning, it will never capture every eventuality.

After all, organisations are dynamic and are continually adapting to market challenges. Therefore, deploying any new initiative does not happen in a vacuum. Although we had developed what we thought were effective plans we needed to adapt to social, political, economic and structural change within Lucent and externally to support customer requirements. Our deployment approach therefore had to evolve into a blend of planned and emerging change to be responsive enough.

We found overcoming the 'metrics' culture a major challenge in particular and, therefore, focused on 'purposeful participation' that created value and believed metric achievement was an outcome and not a goal.

As KM guru David Snowden says, when a measure becomes a goal it is no longer a good measure. Therefore we tried to develop a 'story' around the value proposition that answered the 'what's in it for me' question and focused on the benefits to all key stakeholders.

The value proposition includes elements of Aristotle's 'the art of rhetoric' (the art or technique of persuasion, in the original Greek). This includes 'ethos' (a credible speaker), 'logos' (the value other organisations derive from KM) and 'pathos' (a call to action – passion and emotion). We are currently trying to evolve the story into Steve Denning's framework. This, however, remains a work in progress.

As with most KM programmes, we struggled to understand how we could generate and exploit both explicit and tacit knowledge, as the Ask Lucent programme is primarily focused on converting the tacit knowledge of the analyst, through codification, into explicit knowledge that can be captured in a knowledgebase.

We realised we were losing a large amount of knowledge associated with the analysts' subjective insight, hunches and mental models. Is it possible to codify such frequently intangible tacit knowledge following Nonaka's widely quoted SECI model, published in his seminal book 'The Knowledge Creating Company'?

We therefore created review teams to validate the content. In this context, the support analysts form the centre of a social network as the technical expert that reviews potential solutions in a 'virtual global team'. As they review content, they gain greater understanding and knowledge, partly through their social interaction and partly by updating solutions to problems, person-to-person, not just via technology.

We hope that informal networks will evolve and analysts' personal networks will be enriched as a result. Phase two of Ask

Lucent was also successful and participation continues to grow. However, we did have to manage a number of challenges along the way:

- Champions often struggled to balance the demands of the role with the demands of their everyday jobs;
- The integration of the knowledgebase with existing tools and the constraint of an English-only platform. This, understandably, was a particularly thorny issue, with staff and customers outside the UK obviously preferring their own language;
- The benefits of Ask Lucent were not immediately apparent because of the need to populate the knowledgebase with mature content. Analysts therefore struggled to understand the long-term gain for their perceived short-term pain;
- Communicate the purpose of the programme in non-KM language – keeping the message in the terms of the analysts, the end-users of the system;
- Providing recognition that sustained the 'new' way of working and was integrated into existing human resources frameworks;
- KM should not be an additional task. It should be 'the way we do things around here';
- Try to create the psychological space and time for analysts to reflect on the problem-resolution process so that they can create highly valuable solutions to problems – it should be okay for them to take time to learn from the problem-resolution process and not feel that they immediately have to take on the next customer problem;
- Capturing customer feedback as rating solutions retrieved is not a prominent activity by customers. Customers provide only about two per cent of the feedback we receive, limiting its value;
- Legal intellectual property issues with customers about sharing knowledge.

As with phase one, we carried out an after-action review after phase two to ensure we captured the key learning and applied that knowledge to the deployment in phase three.

The final phase

As with phases one and two, we worked through the plan, act, observe and reflect cycle when we deployed the programme. From the learning activity in phase two, we had a streamlined deployment plan for the champion community to review with their respective teams.

We presented the programme to senior management in the respective countries and began executing the plan. The deployment involved a mixture of online meetings and face-to-face communication, where possible.

Throughout phase three we began to gain a clearer understanding that we needed to improve our content structure to reflect the 'search behaviour' of users. For example, different nationalities use very different search terms to find the same answer. Our solution was therefore to incorporate content that matches the search strings commonly used by various nationalities to try and ensure that solutions are findable for everyone who uses the system.

Many KM initiatives fail because those who could contribute most believe that 'knowledge is power' and are, therefore, reluctant to share. We are working to overcome this challenge by providing recognition for the re-use of content. That is to say, an analyst whose solutions were heavily re-used would be recognised, which

Measuring the Value of Knowledge Management — Chapter 13

would highlight his or her subject-matter expertise within the community.

Knowledge sharing provides 'power' within the community and in a technological environment, too – today's knowledge goes out of date very quickly. The recognition approach requires a shift from an individualised worldview to a collaborative-working model where 'not invented here' syndromes are slowly reconciled with collaborative problem solving – a reasonable mountain to climb.

The sustainability of KM is often questioned as organisations look for bottom-line value – where is the tangible result? We tried to address the issue of value by developing a balanced scorecard that provided information on four areas:

- Operational efficiency – impact on time to solve problems when reusing content;
- KM activity measures – are analysts following the knowledge-centric approach?
- Customer activity – are customers solving problems through self-service?
- Financial impact – savings from customer self-service and analyst re-use of content.

ROI and other benefits

The balanced scorecard provided a broad perspective on the value of the Ask Lucent programme to the organisation and demonstrated achievement of the business goals. As with any KM programme, putting a price on savings made or revenue generated is one of the challenges we need to overcome to demonstrate the importance of KM as a discipline.

We soon began to see the collaboration between units in Lucent that historically had worked on a silo basis increase as we started to overcome geographical dispersion through effective knowledge generation and transfer. The ability of the organisation to capture and re-use knowledge to reduce rework and duplication of effort, including customer self-serving, provided Lucent with substantial – and broadly measurable – operational efficiencies. We still have a way to go, however, although the benefits are becoming very persuasive. During 2005 we achieved the following benefits:

- A 30 per cent reduction in the average time taken to solve customer problems through the re-use of content;
- The use of self-service by customers has been growing every month;
- The number of escalations have been cut by 10 percent;
- 1.5 million in estimated savings generated through increased use of customer self-service and efficiency gains in-house;
- A support organisation more focused on the importance of leveraging knowledge.

The Ask Lucent deployment presented many challenges. However, focusing on the importance of knowledge and embedding the knowledge activity into the daily work practices of the analysts played an important role in legitimising the Ask Lucent programme, fuelling wider adoption.

Demonstrating the value of effective KM on a continual basis and communicating success were key enablers. Moreover, we understood that not all knowledge can be managed and only through providing appropriate 'enablers' will the knowledge asset of a company grow.

Simon Walker is a business manager at Lucent Technologies based in the UK. He can be contacted at swalker1@lucent.com

14. A competency-based framework for knowledge and learning

The following extracts from 'Tools for Knowledge and Learning: A guide for development and humanitarian organisations' by Ben Ramalingam, Knowledge and Learning Specialist at the Overseas Development Institute, demonstrate the critical role of measurement and evaluation in developing and implementing a coherent KM strategy in the not-for-profit sector.

THE OVERSEAS Development Institute (ODI) is Britain's leading independent think-tank on international development and humanitarian issues. Our mission is to inspire and inform policy and practice which lead to the reduction of poverty, the alleviation of suffering and the achievement of sustainable livelihoods in developing countries. We do this by locking together high-quality applied research, practical policy advice, and policy-focused dissemination and debate. We work with partners in the public and private sectors, in both developing and developed countries. ODI's work centres on its research and policy groups and programmes.

The idea of capturing, storing and sharing knowledge so as to learn lessons from the past and from elsewhere – overcoming the boundaries posed by time and space – is far from being a new one. In recent years, a growing movement has emphasised the improved application of knowledge and learning as a means to improve development and humanitarian work. The movement has led to the widespread adoption of learning and knowledge-based strategies among the range of agencies involved in such work, including donor agencies, multilaterals, non-government organisations (NGOs), research institutes, and the plethora of institutions based in the South, including national governments, regional organisations, and indigenous NGOs.

Tools for Knowledge and Learning: A guide for development and humanitarian organisations is a KM toolkit produced by ODI and aimed at staff working in all such organisations. It contains 30 tools and techniques divided into five categories: (1) Strategy Development; (2) Management Techniques; (3) Collaboration Mechanisms; (4) Knowledge Sharing and Learning Processes; and (5) Knowledge Capture and Storage.

Many of these tools are simple and trying them out requires nothing more than the desire to try something new, and the drive to 'get on and do it'. Undertaking them effectively requires effective – sometimes advanced – facilitation and communication skills. Here, we have aimed to provide comprehensive accounts of how to apply such techniques, with a focus on the requirements of potential facilitators. Other tools are more complex, and call for significant planning and resources if they are to be delivered effectively.

There are a number of existing toolkits on knowledge and learning, some of which, such as the deservedly popular UK National Health Service KM toolkit and the *Learning to Fly* books, have served as inspiration for the current volume.

The aim behind this toolkit is to present entry points and references to the wide range of tools and methods that have been used to facilitate improved knowledge and learning in the development and humanitarian sectors.

The RAPID programme

Knowledge and learning is at the heart of the Research and Policy in Development (RAPID) approach on which ODI has been working for the past five years. RAPID has worked hard to further understanding in this area of work, through efforts to deepen awareness of what works in practice, to explore new and innovative ways to apply this awareness, and to undertake action and theoretical research across a wide range of circumstances. Our interest has led us far and wide.

RAPID has undertaken reviews of knowledge and information approaches: a review of information systems in sustainable livelihoods, followed by a literature review of KM and organisational learning and a case-study based investigation into the effectiveness of knowledge and learning.

Valuable lessons have been learned through developing and implementing the ODI strategy for knowledge and learning. RAPID has carried out similar activities for a range of other organisations, including bilateral donor agencies, multilaterals, Southern NGOs and governments.

RAPID has evaluated and suggested improvements to ongoing initiatives, and run training courses for recipient groups ranging from humanitarian workers to economic researchers.

Studies have been made of shifts in international policy on development and humanitarian issues, including examining the contribution of different forms of knowledge to these changes.

RAPID has consulted with civil society organisations across the world as to how they use knowledge to influence policy.

RAPID has facilitated energetic regional and national debates on how to build local capacities to utilise different kinds of knowledge for developmental ends.

We have learned that, regardless of the institutional setting, organisational learning and KM that are successful are those that focus on a number key of organisational competencies.

RAPID research has shown that knowledge and learning tools, if effectively applied, have the potential to transform the efficiency and effectiveness of development and humanitarian agencies. However, tools and techniques alone are not enough: a number of other factors need consideration.

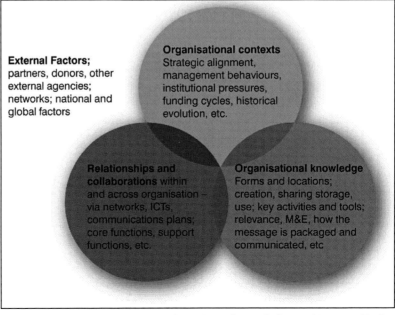

Figure 1: A Holistic View of Knowledge and Learning Tools

Measuring the Value of Knowledge Management Chapter 14

Findings have indicated in particular that where knowledge tools and processes, relationships and collaborations, organisational contextual factors and external factors are dealt with in an integrated and coherent manner, resulting strategies may prove more effective. Since undertaking this research, we have applied these principles in wide range of settings, learning more with each application.

Figure 1, above, developed as part of our research into this area, demonstrates the importance of using knowledge and learning tools as part of a holistic approach to organisational change. The diagram takes account of the specific environment and pressures faced by development and humanitarian agencies. The knowledge, relationships, contexts, external factors model is one that has since been used by RAPID to undertake research on existing initiatives and to develop new initiatives. And as the test of any such model is in the application, we have been gratified that it has proved useful in a range of settings.

ODI's strategic approach

Our approach was inspired and has been reinforced by the groundbreaking and highly popular work of Chris Collison and Geoff Parcell in their *Learning to Fly* series. In particular, we have found their Five Competencies Framework very useful in organising and applying tools within KM and organisational learning initiatives. We believe that the approach addresses a fundamental need in knowledge and learning: the need for a conceptual framework such that the different dimensions of such an initiative can be simply communicated and easily understood.

We have used the model presented in Figure 1 to adapt the Five Competencies Framework, and have been encouraging organisations to use this as a starting point for developing their own knowledge and learning strategies. Groups and teams can easily apply the process to work out how well they are performing in terms of the Five Competencies, and identify their goals and priorities for improvement.

Strategy development

The following tools relate to how an organisation might start to look at its knowledge and learning in a strategic manner and provide different frameworks which can be used to plan, monitor and evaluate knowledge and learning initiatives.

- **The Five Competencies Framework** – This serves as a starting point to help establish clear rationale and entry points for using this toolkit.
- **Knowledge Audit** – Knowledge Audit provides a structure for gathering data, synthesising findings and making recommendations about the best way forward for knowledge and learning initiatives against a background of the broader structural, operational and policy factors affecting an organisation.
- **Social Network Analysis** – Social Network Analysis (SNA) has been called the most systematic way of analysing relationships and knowledge flows between individuals and groups. Properly undertaken, SNA can yield invaluable data about how to tailor and focus knowledge and learning activities to organisational needs.
- **Most Significant Change** – Most Significant Change is a narrative-based mechanism for planning programmes of change. As so much of knowledge and learning is about change, and this change takes place in a variety of different domains, the MSC tool could prove invaluable.

	Strategy development	Management techniques	Collaboration mechanisms	Knowledge sharing and learning	Knowledge capture and storage
Level 5 (high)	Knowledge and learning are integral parts of the overall organisational strategy. A set of tools is available and well communicated, and the capacity to apply them is actively strengthened.	Managers and leaders recognise and reinforce the link between knowledge, learning and performance. Managers regularly apply the relevant tools and techniques, and act as learning role models. Staff ToRs contain references to knowledge sharing and learning.	Collaboration is a defining principle across the organisation. A range of internal and external collaboration mechanisms operate, with clearly defined roles and responsibilities in terms of the organisational goals. Some have clear external deliverables while others develop capability in the organisation.	Prompts for learning are built into key processes… Programme staff routinely find out who knows what, inside and outside the organisation, and talk with them. A common language, templates and guidelines support effective sharing.	Information is easy to access and retrieve. Selected information is sent to potential users in a systematic and coherent manner. High priority information assets have multiple managers who are responsible for updating, summarising and synthesising information. Exit interviews and handovers are used systematically.
Level 4	A knowledge and learning strategy exists, but is not integrated with overall goals. A set of tools for knowledge and learning is available and understood by most staff.	Management view knowledge and learning as everyone's responsibility. Managers increasingly ask for and exhibit learning approaches. There are rewards and incentives for using such approaches.	Networks are organised around business needs. They have a clear governance document, and utilise supportive technology. External parties are included in some networks.	'Learning before, during and after is the way things are done around here.' Beneficiaries and partners participate in review sessions. External knowledge plays a role in shaping projects.	Key information is kept current and easily accessible. One individual acts as the guardian of each information asset, and encourages people to contribute. Many do.
Level 3	There are ongoing discussions about developing a knowledge and learning strategy. A wide range of tools are being used across the organisation.	Knowledge and learning is viewed as the responsibility of a specific role or roles. Some managers talk the talk, but don't always walk the walk!	People are using networks and working groups to get results. Peers are helping peers across organisational boundaries. Formal collaboration mechanisms are being created and recognised.	People can find out what the organisation knows. Some examples of sharing and learning are highlighted and recognised across the organisation. Some information translates across boundaries.	Specific groups take responsibility for their own information and file it in one location in a common format for easy access. Searching information assets before starting activities is encouraged, as is sharing lessons afterwards. Some handovers take place.

Figure 2: Matrix for the Five Competencies Framework

Measuring the Value of Knowledge Management — Chapter 14

Level 2	Many people say that sharing knowledge is important to the organisation's success. Some people are using some tools to help with learning and sharing.	Some managers give people the time to share and learn, but there is little visible support from the top.	Ad hoc personal networking is used by individuals who know each other to achieve goals. This is increasingly recognised as vital to the organisation.	People learn before doing and programme review sessions. They sometimes capture what they learn for the purpose of sharing, but in practice few do access it.	A few groups capture lessons learned after a project, and look for information before starting a project. There is potential access to lots of information, but it is not summarised.
Level 1 (basic)	A few people express that knowledge is important to the organisation. Isolated individuals begin to talk about how important – and difficult – it is.	Knowledge and learning are viewed with scepticism. Management think learning leads to lack of accountability. 'Knowledge is power' at the highest levels of the organisation.	Knowledge hoarders seem to get rewarded. There are few cross-cutting collaborations. Silos are hard to break down.	People are conscious of the need to learn from what they do, but rarely get the time. Sharing is for the benefit of specific teams.	Some individuals take the time to capture their lessons, but do so in a confusing variety of formats. Most don't contribute to information assets, and even fewer search them. No exit interviews or handovers take place.

Figure 2 continued

- **Outcome Mapping** – Outcome Mapping (OM) is a participatory planning, monitoring and evaluation methodology which focuses on the contribution of a programme to changes in the actions and behaviours of the 'boundary partners'. Applied to knowledge and learning strategies, OM has a number of potential benefits.
- **Scenario Testing and Visioning** – These tools focus on the future of an organisation, and enable imaginative and creative ideas to play a central role in developing and rolling out knowledge strategies.

The starting point – or the overall framework for the ODI's KM toolkit – is the Five Competencies Framework, which is described in more detail in the following paragraphs.

The Five Competencies Framework
Introduction

In the influential book *Learning to Fly*, Chris Collison and Geoff Parcell (2001) describe five key organisational 'competencies'. As already stated, we see these being of high practical relevance for KM and organisational learning initiatives. The Five Competencies Framework has been promoted widely and is now being used by many different teams or groups to work out how well they are performing against organisationally established criteria for knowledge and learning, and to identify goals and priorities for improvement. The competency framework works on the principle that effective knowledge and learning is based on improving performance in five important competency areas:

- Strategy development;
- Management techniques;

> **Case Study: CARE International**
>
> As part of a Partnership Programme Agreement (awarded by the Department for International Development), CARE International UK was looking to develop four regional networks, focusing on HIV/AIDS, private sector partnerships (PPPs), international financial institutions (IFIs) and civil society organisations (CSOs).
>
> As part of a two-day training course to help with the knowledge and learning aspects of this work, the CARE team was introduced to the five competencies approach, as well as a number of other tools that would help build capacity in each area. Following this, the team decided to run a KM strategy session as part of a five-day conference in Quito, Ecuador, under the PPP theme. The core of this was to explain the Five Competencies Framework, and to get participants to think through where the network was at present, and where it wanted to be. The workshop proved to be a resounding success with participants, and laid the groundwork for the operation of the network in the future.

- Collaboration mechanisms;
- Knowledge sharing and learning processes;
- Knowledge capture and storage.

Based on these competencies, Parcell and Collison developed a framework to be worked through by groups and teams within a given organisation. This framework can be used to discover how well teams or groups believe they are performing against the pre-established criteria, and where they most wish to improve.

Detailed description of the process

The Five Competencies Framework is an exercise enabling an organisation (or a group of organisations) to work out, in a simple and effective manner, what different elements have to learn and what they have to share in the realm of organisational learning and KM. Importantly, the framework also provides a common framework and language to support the knowledge and learning, and can also be used to connect people with something to share to people with something to learn.

For each of the five competency areas outlined above, the framework describes five levels of performance, from basic to high. The framework is therefore a five-by-five matrix (see Figure 2). The first step is to get a group of stakeholders from across an organisation or team to work together to discuss relative strengths and areas for improvement in terms of knowledge and learning. The group should work to determine the Current level for each of the competencies and the Target level for each. The idea is to get the statement that best describes the organisation. The target should be determined by projecting some reasonable time into the future – say, two years. The framework can also be used to determine the priorities for immediate action, through selection of the competency area which will yield greatest benefits if improved.

Key points/practical tips

As stated in the introduction, this tool can be used to establish clear entry points and rationale for applying a range of KM tools.

It is also a very good tool to support the improved communication and understanding of knowledge and learning strategies.

Sources and further reading
Collison, C. and Parcell G., (2001) *Learning to Fly*, Oxford: Capstone Publishing, Inc. This tool has been adapted following applications by the author in a range of different settings in the development and humanitarian sectors.

Ben Ramalingam, knowledge and learning specialist, is a member of the Research and Policy in Development (RAPID) Programme at the Overseas Development Institute in London. He provides advice and support to a wide range of international development and humanitarian agencies, from United Nations international agencies to local civil society organisations. He can be contacted at b.ramalingam@odi.org.uk

15. A debate on monitoring and evaluating KM activities

KM for Development (KM4Dev) is a community of international development practitioners who are interested in KM and knowledge sharing issues and approaches. Ben Ramalingam outlines the three distinct levels apparent in the various discussions about KM-related monitoring and evaluation that have taken place on the KM4Dev platform over the last few years.

THE *FIRST* level of the discussions focused on monitoring and evaluation within KM activities. These largely related to numerical summaries of outputs. For example, one member asked for ways of monitoring electronic discussions and online chats, and collated the following as useful indicators:

- For electronic discussions:
  - User transaction reports (to see when members visit the CoP site, etc);
  - Number of comments/posts, etc;
  - Lurk to post ratio;
  - Document creation and upload to libraries/archives/lessons learned/databases, etc;
  - Qualitative results from surveys.
- For online chats:
  - Unique Chat Hosts;
  - Unique Chat User;
  - Unique Active Chat User;
  - Unique Chat User Duration.

Similar indicators were more geared towards specific knowledge strategies, and focused on ways of tracking the utilisation of knowledge and learning tools, for example:

- Use of intranet, tracking things like hits;
- Application of After-Action Review (AAR) and Peer Assists in projects;
- Number of informal knowledge sharing sessions;
- Number of exit interviews and handovers.

All of the above might be usefully tracked as percentages, i.e. percentage of projects with AARs, etc.

The *second level* focused on the difficulties of monitoring and evaluating the impact of KM strategies. Here the discussion focused less on solutions and more on how difficult this kind of monitoring actually proves to be in practice.

There were obvious practical issues – for example, how do you track the utilisation of a single AAR, let alone a library of AARs? There were also some conceptual issues which were to do with the nature of knowledge as an inherently unmeasurable aspect of organisational life.

Managerial difficulties were also highlighted. Specifically, there is a need to align knowledge and learning with overall organisational objectives, but knowledge and learning often calls for business strategy to be scrutinised and questioned from multiple angles. This leads to a tension which isn't easily resolved. Finally, these activities carry time and cost implications in terms of collection and storage of information related to knowledge and learning. It is frequently hard enough to get users to apply KM approaches – asking for careful and consistent monitoring is seen by some as asking for too much. One way of resolving this was to focus on information which had true management impact. But this was also problematic. As one contributor put it, "Knowledge is in the eye of the beholder, and different people have different needs in terms of information quality, quantity and timeliness."

Finally, the *third level* of discussion related to the potential application of knowledge and learning for monitoring and evaluating the overall impact of development. Here the key question was whether KM strategies should focus less on the performance of KM programmes, or the impact of KM on organisations, and more on the impact of knowledge on developmental results. This raised the issue of the cultural and intellectual pillars of evaluation, and how this has a fundamental impact on what knowledge is seen as 'appropriate' or 'useful' for development.

Specifically, it was suggested that the explicit or implicit premise of knowledge management is that judgements and decisions that are based on certain kinds of evidence, information, and analysis are superior to others. However, in the development environment, there is seldom a solid, irrefutable case for any particular decision – this is true in public policy generally, but is heightened in the international aid world.

Despite this difficulty, development practitioners value plans and budgets and proposals that are grounded in facts, credible evidence, well argued analogies from similar situations, building from credible theories with convincing success stories, pilot projects that were successful and merit 'scaling up' with or without modifications, etc. We frown upon proposals to the extent that they lack these attractive qualities even if they are attractive plausible visions of charismatic leaders who are able to inspire a group to action based on other factors such as religious faith, political expediency, cronyism, and desperation for lack of alternatives.

As hinted at earlier, the issue is not specific to development, but universal, and can be summarised as finding an effective bridge between the social sciences and management decision-making. KM might be of most help in initiatives such as following up the Monterey Statement, in collating common approaches and lessons learned on how donor organisations and partners track and monitor development results and impact. In this context, it was thought that KM should point to the importance of diversity and robustness of approaches to monitoring and evaluation. Specifically, there should not be an attempt to reduce all approaches to a standard mechanism which is determined by those with the largest funds to allocate for developmental purposes.

It was suggested, in light of the debate, that the potential of KM is not to simply support the impact of development, but also question how development is undertaken. Such an approach runs the risk of "trying to improve the quality of a car's gauges without repairing the engine."

Ben Ramalingam, knowledge and learning specialist, is a member of the Research and Policy in Development (RAPID) Programme at the Overseas Development Institute in London. He provides advice and support to a wide range of international development and humanitarian agencies, from United Nations international agencies to local civil society organisations. He can be contacted at b.ramalingam@odi.org.uk

16. Ricardo: Driven by knowledge

Martin Ward explores the processes, principles and constraints influencing the sustained success of a company that depends on knowledge to survive.

WHAT FOLLOWS is an (inevitably selective) insider's view of how a company that thrives on knowledge alone – we manufacture prototypes, or at most low-volume products, and depend on consultancy for most of our income – is achieving competitive success in a sector that is permanently racked by overproduction, crises of quality and confidence, a steadfast habit of restructuring at all levels, and tight margins for all participants. We don't exactly live on air in the motor industry, but it feels like it sometimes.

The knowledge-driven nature of Ricardo's contribution to the industries it serves will be obvious to the reader even from the thumbnail sketch of the company that is provided in the sidebar. Ricardo's basic aims have never varied: to acquire knowledge (input knowledge), process it and generate from it a range of knowledge products and services (output knowledge) that match or anticipate the changing needs of our clients. This article attempts to illuminate these basic aims as the company pursues them today, noting in addition the key contribution of non-knowledge-based factors that are essential to every company's survival and success.

Sources of input knowledge

There is such a thing as new knowledge, but all knowledge advances imply development from some existing base. Every graduate who joins us has acquired formal, publicly available knowledge, in an environment largely concerned with knowledge for the sake of knowledge. Once inside Ricardo, the graduate will work with knowledge for the sake of profit. While it is unlikely that an engineer who cannot handle the fundamental issues of engineering as a discipline will make much commercial impact, such issues are no longer their main concern, even though good research and methodological skills are essential to Ricardo's work.

Input knowledge is also obtained from testing and measuring engineering products belonging to Ricardo or its clients under various controlled conditions, and with a variety of specific knowledge outcomes in mind. While the outcomes may fulfil contractual requirements, they will also be logged in Ricardo's own files and records. Ricardo's long-term ambition is to integrate the engine data acquired in this way into a commercially useful system of benchmarking, although the practical difficulties involved remain unsolved so far.

Ricardo has occasionally had to set up offices on its own site to house confidential client projects from which no information is supposed to escape, but this provision cannot apply to the Ricardo engineers directly involved, and generalised forms of the results obtained have been known to find their way into common internal knowledge. The need to work for a number of companies simultaneously, between which there may be fierce competition, leads to tricky problems of site management and administrative confidentiality.

Other ways of building input knowledge include hiring experts, either temporarily as consultants or permanently as employees, and acquiring entire companies, as Ricardo has done several times in the course of constructing its global divisions. This type of knowledge is already well on its way to commercial fruitfulness, and has the momentum that is otherwise so difficult to generate in a wholly new department or project.

Other essential forms of input knowledge include general knowledge, without which neither firms nor individuals can operate, and what one might call 'maintenance knowledge', the common stock of legal, financial and administrative knowledge and skills that firms need if they are to remain within the law and to work efficiently. This knowledge is usually evaluated by external bodies for quality-assurance purposes, which are increasingly important in acquiring business from clients. Like every other company, Ricardo keeps a watchful eye on competitors and potential clients, as well as the often painful workings of the motor industry as a whole.

Taming input knowledge

In the most general terms, Ricardo's engineers, in the course of their everyday work, either acquire or process input knowledge, and turn it into knowledge products and services. They then effectively sell the latter to clients. The following section discusses the ways in which input knowledge is processed.

Real, profitable knowledge has to be assimilated by individuals to the point that they can identify with it completely. This could not happen without some degree of prior grounding, reflecting the principle that knowledge always has antecedents. Not everything has to be internalised; no-one could contemplate digesting endless columns of test results. Knowledge involves a grasp of principles, while data supports this knowledge in specific forms. While human beings are highly capable of grasping broad principles of a subject, there are severe limits to their abilities to cope with data. The processing and storing of data is best left to computers, files and reference books.

If knowledge is not really knowledge until it has been assimilated, it is hard to fully accept Karl Popper's account of 'objective knowledge' being divorced from consciousness. At Ricardo, people are key to the acquisition, assimilation, transfer and use of knowledge. Individuals inevitably have their own subjective viewpoints, as well as prejudices, temperaments, preferences, susceptibilities and lopsided talents. Yet they also have insights, and things occur to them spontaneously and in ways that no machine could ever hope emulate. People's minds often go on working on problems after hours; people can summarise their existing knowledge succinctly and swiftly; people generate innovations and create judgements that are relevant to novel circumstances.

Paradoxically, the objectivity of formal knowledge, and its commercial progeny, depends on its independence from individual circumstances and histories. Given a specific, standard technical problem, we would expect all qualified engineers to come up with a similar solution. The integrity of objective knowledge has to survive personality. It is written into the professional mind.

Achieving competitive knowledge

The aim of assimilating and processing input knowledge is what might be described as 'competitive knowledge', which enables the firm both to survive and to succeed in the highly competitive industry in which Ricardo operates. There are a number of roughly equivalent knowledge-based companies to which clients could turn to achieve their

Measuring the Value of Knowledge Management

aims; Ricardo's ambition is to attract as much of this work as possible.

Given this, innovation remains very much at the centre of Ricardo's quest for competitive knowledge. The company's R&D department clearly plays an important role here; the products it produces are often the crown jewels of the company. Every knowledge company has a lurking wish to hit on an idea so astounding that its competitors will be knocked flat, for example an engine that only needs air as fuel. Unfortunately, experience shows that, in the motor industry at least, the more spectacular the idea, the more likely it is to conflict with existing industry infrastructures. These have usually been developed painfully and at great expense over decades, and motor-industry leaders, not keen to see their investment compromised, will think very hard before buying into anything really revolutionary. The wonderful idea is thus denied commercial success. Private inventors can never understand why their brainwaves do not take the world by storm; Ricardo's experts, often asked to assist them, usually do. Even lesser brainwaves, which initially promise to reach some long-held industry Oily Grail, have frequently fallen flat for the same reason. Radical innovation in this field equates to high risk.

The motor industry does not deal in paradigm shifts, whereby a whole generation of work is rendered obsolete overnight by a single startling announcement, as in the world of pure science. Rather, commercial innovation is usually incremental. The most productive idea for a knowledge company may be one that significantly advances an already apparent industry trend, in which everyone agrees there is a good commercial future. A prime recent example is Ricardo's mild hybrid car the i-MoGen (Intelligent Motor Generator), which hit the spot with the industry at the time of its launch.

Successful innovation in the motor industry often comes in piecemeal form via 'enabling' ideas, which operate in the field of commonly recognised problems. For example, a better mousetrap is worth more to us than a wholly mechanical cat. Equally, innovation in the motor industry is often more illusion than reality. Many of the current technologies that seem so exciting, such as direct-injection gasoline engines, have in fact been around for decades, held back by a lack of enabling technologies, which in recent years have generally been provided by developments in electronics, a field that really lies outside the province of the motor industry. Many knowledge companies, particularly those in the engine-components business, have succeeded by finally realising these well established ideas.

There are few genuine dead ends when it comes to a knowledge business, and profit often flows from old discoveries. Ricardo's archive of old company reports is one of the most heavily used sources of information. Even faintly new ideas usually come in waves of parallel developments, filling the industry with slightly different versions of the same idea, particularly in the transmissions business.

Knowledge products and services

The result of processing input knowledge is knowledge products, in essence anything a client will agree to purchase. A knowledge product can be a prototype, component or model; a semi-tangible good such as a report, a design drawing or a piece of information; a licence to use a concept protected by a patent; or, a vital piece of software. These are the kinds of knowledge products that Ricardo has thrived on for over 70 years. Nowadays, Ricardo's Information

Chapter 16 — *Measuring the Value of Knowledge Management*

> **About Ricardo**
>
> Ricardo was founded in 1917 by Sir Harry Ricardo, an eminent engineer who pioneered studies of engine combustion, fuels and octane rating, and designed and patented many combustion and other engine systems. The company has never lost its knowledge-leadership status in the motor industry, and today continues to provide clients throughout the world with innovations, consultancy and technical expertise. It works through its major divisions at Shoreham-by-Sea, Cambridge and Leamington Spa in the UK, sizeable divisions in the US and Germany, and offices in Japan, China, Korea, India and Italy. Ricardo makes a significant contribution to the flow of knowledge in the industries it serves via its world-class Information Services Department, based in Shoreham, which is a unique example of a largely self-financing information service. For more information, visit www.ricardo.com.

Services Department (ISD) sells its own knowledge products, such as newsletters, copies of publicly available papers and articles, lists of references or translations.

Clients are prepared to pay, so long as they can see how far Ricardo has developed the input knowledge from its original state. The quality and speed of the company's work are what gives us an edge over our rivals. One of Ricardo's engineering departments that serves clients in this way is the Technical Support Service (TSS), which co-ordinates the knowledge of engineers throughout the company to answer specific technical questions from clients who subscribe to the service via a technical-support agreement.

The difference between the output of the TSS and the ISD may sometimes be hard to detect. The TSS makes heavy use of the knowledge acquired, stored and organised by ISD, and members of the TSS are not always asked to be particularly original in their answers to clients. If clients are dealing with an area of knowledge that relates to one with which they are already familiar, they will be prepared to pay for fairly generalised but conveniently packaged summaries of the state of the art in the new field.

Another essential component of commercial knowledge provision as a whole is the understanding (which may be explicit) that the client is given exclusive access to that knowledge; this would not be the case with knowledge that is easily accessible to everyone, for instance over the internet, and can only be assured by conditions of confidentiality. On the other hand, the ISD provides a great deal of publicly available knowledge, but clients are prepared to pay because of the value added by convenient and reliable presentation, which saves them hours of time.

Irrespective of the type of product on offer, though, it is important for a knowledge company to always to be on the look out for novel products, as well as new ways in which its products can be presented and communicated. The advent of the worldwide web has opened up whole new possibilities in this respect, and every new development in ICT should be seen as an opportunity to amend or extend a company's portfolio, particularly if the development implies the obsolescence of an existing communications medium.

Knowledge services may be rather less tangible than knowledge products. They

Measuring the Value of Knowledge Management — Chapter 16

Lessons learnt

The following points should strike a chord with readers who work for consultancies:

- Take careful note of the characteristics of the industry you work in. The motor industry is a mature one, in which radically new knowledge (if it is still possible) is unlikely to thrive. Nothing that will really upset the status quo has a chance of succeeding. The most fruitful kind of competitive knowledge will have other roles than revolution – such as enablement, canny extensions of existing trends, tidying up dead ends, complementing, supporting, providing variants, repackaging, updating, standardising and so on. Be prepared to replace any innovations with others that are equally good, because no monopoly is forever;
- Note Ricardo's global spread, both knowledge-wise and geographically, which presents numerous chances for success in different areas and markets – not every division will be on top all of the time. Also, this allows for a wide spread of clients, and the ability to service them on their doorsteps. Be protean; no job is too small.

Readers who work for organisations that rely on physical products can also learn from us:

- The management of anything includes the management of knowledge; in this sense, we are all knowledge managers. The recognition of the role of subjective factors (insight, originality, creativity, inventiveness) and their unwanted shadows (prejudice, resistance to change, inflexibility) must be balanced against the need to preserve objectivity, accuracy, fidelity – the qualities of knowledge for its own sake – if knowledge is to lead to profit;
- Whether you are talking about strategy, management, product research and selection, product design, development and testing, product manufacture, marketing, distribution, or aftermarket service, or the complementary skills of site management, accountancy and legal services, nothing is immune from knowledge-based analysis, from the impact of knowledge or from the benefit of creativity. Striving for monopoly is the same as with a knowledge-only company, as is the certainty that the monopoly will wither; both types of company need to replace competitive knowledge, to repackage it, to communicate it in new forms, and to add variants and improvements in order to stay ahead;
- All companies depend on qualities that are not directly concerned with knowledge: careful management, a positive company culture, state-of-the-art plant and facilities, and the care of clients, involving the preservation of trust and loyalty, confidentiality and value for money.

include the use of advanced testing and other facilities, including databases provided by the ISD on a subscription basis, knowledge transfer in the form of seminars, presentations and training courses (including on-site training and initiation of client employees), and secondment, recruitment and placement services. In recent years, Ricardo's Strategic Consulting division has added to this list the provision of high-level strategic advice to major manufacturing and other companies. Every knowledge service requires an infrastructure that itself reflects the state of the art.

Much of Ricardo's bread and butter work consists of applying engineering knowledge to the solution of problems raised by projects that the company contracts to carry out for a client. These projects may involve the design and development of new products, or the revision of existing products that are obsolete, underpowered or faulty. While none of these tasks could be done by non-engineers, the amount of new engineering knowledge, judgement and insight required varies considerably, as does the length and difficulty of each project. Not all Ricardo's work takes place at the frontiers of knowledge.

Indeed, the provision of knowledge products and services is not the end of the story. As in any business, good relationships between Ricardo and its clients are critical, as is the reputation of the firm. At the same time, no monopoly lasts for ever. Ricardo has to be ready to replace its competitive knowledge with new, equally competitive ideas. The speed with which competitive knowledge can be generated and replaced is a key factor in the firm's ongoing success. It is a ruthless and relentless process, but Ricardo's success in moulding itself as a knowledge company means it is well placed to maintain its competitive status. Having shared some of the processes, principles and constraints that go with being a knowledge company like Ricardo, our hope is that other companies will be able to derive an improved understanding of the factors that will influence and enable their own success in this field.

The analysis presented in this case study is an entirely personal one, and does not reflect view of the company as a whole.

Martin Ward is an information specialist with Ricardo Consulting Engineers. He can be contacted at martin.ward@ricardo.com

17. Identifying Ricardo's knowledge assets

IT WOULD be desirable to present our knowledge assets in such a way that their status at different points in time can be compared, and that they can be compared with those of other companies, requirements which suggest a quantitative approach as far as possible.

The extent to which knowledge assets can be quantified, and, though real in their contribution to profit, cannot be quantified but must be suggested or presented in conceptual form, is a matter of controversy. The following is an attempt to identify the types of knowledge assets which Ricardo possesses, prior to an attempt to give each, where possible, a numerical value.

Distinguishing knowledge from other assets

It may be cooking the books to insist that, as Ricardo is a knowledge company and depends on knowledge for its profitability, ALL its assets subserve Ricardo's knowledge activity, and are therefore, directly or indirectly, knowledge assets.

This would account for the bricks and mortar, physical and real estate assets we possess. The latter very soon merge into direct knowledge assets, e.g. test rigs, production facilities, stores, conference rooms, housekeeping facilities, library areas and furniture, laboratory equipment, office equipment and accessories and computer hardware, which represent the immediate and indispensable infrastructure for knowledge activities. So, in practice, the difficulty in separating these assets from those which do not contribute directly to knowledge activities, such as company vehicles (apart from test vehicles), car parks, gardens, sewage plants and fuel farms, tends to support the assertion that all our assets are, in a greater or less immediate fashion, knowledge assets.

> **Suggested metrics**
> - No. of test beds
> - Laboratory facilities
> - No. of PCs
> - No. of laptops
> - No. of email addresses
> - No. of Internet access points
> - No. of Intranet access points
> - No. of telephones
> - No. of conference rooms
> - No. of photocopiers
> - No. of printers
> - No. of servers

Intangible

Intangible and completely unquantifiable knowledge assets are mainly represented by the depth of history which, through many upheavals and discontinuities, has produced the company we have today. Both client history, and the impact of Ricardo's own knowledge workers, remembered and forgotten, over nearly the last 100 years, form a real but unmeasurable and often indefinable set of precursors for our current knowledge state, and at the same time give us a definite competitive edge over our less historically-grounded competitors. More concretely, e.g. in the form of memories, objects and documents, we possess the past achievements of the company in our present working lives. Objects and documents can be counted and catalogued, and passed on or shown to enquiring clients, while memories are truly intangible, but represent an essential resource when trying to reconstruct the past, as is sometimes required by long-standing clients.

> **Suggested metrics**
> - Depth of history in years
> - No. of pensioners

Archives
One set of working documents from the past is the archive of old test results, stored both on and off site. This represents a record of work in the immediate past which has to be kept for legal reasons, but is a resource much used by engineers, as is the Library's collection of paper or microfilmed copies of internal reports reaching back well into the past. Perhaps less frequently used, though when used often producing high value results, is the Library's store of old periodicals and books.

> **Suggested metrics**
> - Archive of past test results: active files
> - Projects covered
> - Closed database of internal reports; number of articles
> - Closed uncatalogued collection of old patents
> - Length of shelves of closed collection of periodicals
> - Length of shelves of closed archive of internal, uncatalogued documents

Patents
Although they are expensive to obtain and maintain, patents are a source of income, £2-300,000 p.a., in terms, for example, of damages won as a result of defending them, and of licensing. They also act as status symbols in a marketing and company image sense. They are also concrete indicators of innovative achievement: Japanese clients in particular are fond of asking about Ricardo's patent portfolio and the number of patents granted per year, when deciding to do business with us. Additionally, they give legal protection to dearly-won ideas and concepts.

The corporate attitude to patents is coloured by the short-term bottom-line approach which sees them as one-offs not justifying long-term investment of resources. In terms of local financial concerns they are often seen as an unwarranted cost and as an irritation/distraction. There is no effective Group-status champion of IP and licensing.

Assimilated knowledge
General knowledge
The 'knowledge in people's heads' is clearly a major asset in our knowledge work. A staff member epitomises a range of knowledge types. These include the general knowledge, including interpersonal and communication skills, without which none of us can operate or cooperate as social beings. Such general knowledge increases with age and experience, and can be acquired by recruitment.

> **Suggested metrics**
> - Total number of staff employed ('general knowledge' community)
> - Total number of staff employed for more than 10 years
> - Number of separate sites and offices internally affording face-to-face working contact, but requiring to be linked by communications media
> - Number of staff recruited
> - Number of leavers

Knowledge of working practices

Also of importance is knowledge of company and working practices, independent of, or parallel to, engineering knowledge. This knowledge is specific to Ricardo and functions, like general knowledge, as a communal possession, enriched and deepened (as well as modified) by time and experience. It cannot be acquired by recruitment.

Metrics: as for General knowledge, above.

Engineering knowledge

The engineering knowledge which staff members possess can be loosely divided into two kinds, the possession of techniques, formulae, procedures, principles, laws and other formal or methodological knowledge; and the possession of specific data, which populates the parameters of the latter structures of formal knowledge. While the residence time of specific data within an individual's mind is likely to be limited, due to the constant flux of experience, this does not apply to formal/methodological knowledge, which characterises engineers as engineers, and which would be expected to survive as a permanent intellectual possession, growing and maturing over time. Without them, engineers would not be engineers.

> **Suggested metrics**
> - No. of qualified engineers currently employed
> - No. of qualified technicians employed
> - No. of staff with PhDs
> - No. of staff with MBAs

Know-how

The practical application of formal knowledge generates 'know-how', the ability to relate theory to practice, which grows in depth and confidence over time: a recent graduate may possess more formal knowledge than some of his or her seniors, but it takes experience and mentoring for this knowledge to be successfully let loose on client projects.

> **Suggested metrics**
> - No. of qualified engineers and technicians with more than five years of working experience
> - No. of formally-appointed mentors

Management skills

Managerial knowledge and skill is a further aspect of working knowledge without which the work of the company could not go forward. The possession of expert and experienced managers gives the company a competitive knowledge edge.

> **Suggested metrics**
> - No. of staff of management grade or above

Non-engineering specialist knowledge

Further knowledge contributions are made by specialists in non-engineering activities which are nevertheless essential to indirectly support our profit-making knowledge activities. These include the skills of lawyers, personnel managers, accountants, librarians and site personnel.

> **Suggested metrics**
> - No. of qualified lawyers
> - No. of qualified HR staff
> - No. of qualified accountants
> - No. of qualified librarians

Engineering specialists

While all engineers and technicians will possess basic, or perhaps much more than basic, formal engineering knowledge, there are degrees of knowledge in this respect. In its PhDs and other unusually highly qualified staff, Ricardo has immediate access to expert knowledge at a very high level. The number of 'boffins' in the company represents a highly competitive knowledge asset, an asset which can be added to by recruitment.

> **Suggested metrics**
> - No. of staff with exceptional engineering qualifications
> - No. of Technical Specialists
> - No. of staff with non-English language skills

The Ricardo Knowledgebase

No-one has ever seen it, but it is an important concept which describes the totality of knowledge which directly or indirectly supports Ricardo's knowledge output in terms of products and services, and hence its profitability. Ricardo lives or dies by its knowledge, which has to be superior to that of both clients and rivals. In practical terms, Ricardo's knowledgebase is coterminous with Ricardo envisaged as a knowledge community.

The walls of the knowledgebase are fuzzy, but it comprises both explicit and tacit knowledge, both knowledge as a commodity, lodged in library books, and knowledge loaded with the value which Ricardo's engineering activities have given it; both knowledge in heads and knowledge on paper; both systematically-recorded knowledge, and floating knowledge in emails and hard drives.

It is the amount and quality of the contents of the KB which gives us our edge, but also requires a certain amount of internal organisation. Meta-knowledge about what we know is an essential key to unlocking the treasures of the KB; conversely, blocks and kinks in communication channels and organisation can hinder the flow of knowledge around the KB and its effective contribution to the knowledge output.

As we have identified the KB with the Ricardo Knowledge Community, some of these kinks and blocks are personal in nature: A not knowing what B has done with client Z; nobody knowing who is the expert in subject P; department D not yielding up a desirable presentation to H who needs it; K declining to share his knowledge as this might reduce his personal value; the absence of M and N unreachably on holiday simultaneously. Some of the blocks are physical/electronic – computer breakdowns, poor mobile phone signals, books removed from the library without being booked out, crashed engines, leaks, missing tools, thefts and 'borrowings', organisational or office arrangements that impede communication and rapport.

Additionally, knowledge is also lost to the KB through the departure of colleagues, or obsolescence.

Tacit knowledge

Some of the knowledge which Ricardo staff assimilate can be replicated as explicit knowledge, to be found somewhere in written records. Knowledge of a more practical kind, without which Ricardo's work would be impossible, does not emulate a text, but is deeply embedded in an individual's personal and often practical skills, the knowledge that is 'caught' and not 'taught'. The possession of such knowledge is evidenced by specific results, and can sometimes be certified by formal qualifications, such as a fitter or welder, for example. Such qualifications imply a rounded possession of the relevant tacit knowledge. But such tacit knowledge is also what all of us possess, to make our individual lives liveable, and is a key feature of the general knowledge already noted.

Suggested metrics
- No. of certificated practically skilled staff employed

Explicit knowledge

While human memory is capacious, there rapidly comes a point when it has to be backed up by written records which provide explicit knowledge. These represent a massive set of knowledge assets, as personal notes and files, files and emails lodged in software stores, books and documents, drawings, graphs, sketches, library catalogue records, memoranda, letters, diaries and journals, and project files and reports. The knowledge in written records falls loosely into the two categories noted above, i.e. formal and methodological on the one hand, and specific data on the other; a technical paper or report will usually present both types in a rich an informative mixture.

While it is possible to quantify the size and depth of libraries, personal files, databases, hard discs, intranets, excel spreadsheets and other stores of explicit knowledge, access to the internet gives the individual a rapid way in to explicit knowledge which is virtually boundless and unquantifiable in extent. In addition, the Information Services Department at Shoreham represents the link between engineers in search of knowledge and the entire world of formal information and knowledge resources which ISD staff members are trained to access.

Suggested metrics
- No. of terabites of stored digital information and data held
- No. of articles in the database of engineering references (acting as a catalogue to the Library maintained by Information Services)
- Library bookstock
- Library stock of separate journal and other articles
- Periodicals currently subscribed to

Embedded knowledge

Ricardo does not display an organogram on its website as this is held to be a strategic knowledge asset. The internal organisation of the company is a key form of embedded knowledge which gives us a competitive edge, as a distillation of the company's experiences, positive and negative, and a product of the company's strategic thinking. Embedded knowledge is difficult to measure, but is reflected in final outcomes, such as profit levels, and intermediate outcomes, such as the ability to quickly form effective teams comprising all the expertise needed to solve a client's problem. Every procedure identified in the staff manuals is a contribution to embedded knowledge.

Conclusion

This has been an attempt to enumerate some of the main types of knowledge assets which Ricardo possesses. The next step will be to quantify them, where possible.

18. KM Scorecards at Unisys

Alex Goodall outlines how Unisys applies a balanced scorecard to KM projects to determine their value and deliver on its overall KM vision. This article is based on his presentation at Ark Group's conference on Measuring and Demonstrating the Value of Knowledge Management in September 2006.

UNISYS IS an IT services company with around 36,000 employees, operating across 100 countries. We help customers secure business operations so they can better focus on opportunities. We do it by creating visibility throughout all layers of our customers' enterprise: exposing cause-and-effect relationships between strategy, business processes, applications and infrastructure.

We combine expertise in consulting, systems integration, outsourcing, infrastructure and server technology, operating in six primary vertical markets worldwide: financial services, public sector, communications, transportation, commercial and media.

Knowledge Management Vision

Knowledge Management (KM) is at the core of business operations at Unisys and its KM vision, illustrated in Figure 1 below, incorporates the entire enterprise, working on three strategic levels: organisation, team and individual.

In order to deliver on its KM objectives, the company has invested in tools and processes that connect people and content to address all processes in the knowledge cycle. These are brought together under the umbrella of the Unisys KM portal – Knowledge.net.

The KM Scorecard

Unisys has developed a KM scorecard, based on the balanced scorecard methodology, to measure the impact and effectiveness of these substantial investments and their added value to the organisation. The rationale behind this approach is:

- To address the expectation that at some point the KM programme will need to justify its existence quantitatively;

Figure 1: KM Vision

The Agile Enterprise		
Organisation	**Team**	**Individual**
Knowledge led	Connected	Empowered
■ Leverage knowledge of 36,000 people to deliver superior solutions to clients	■ Common purpose, goals and commitment	■ Knowledge of role, responsibilities, priorities, assignments
■ Culture of innovation, learning, sharing and improvement	■ Cross geography, culture and enterprise collaboration	■ Instant access to the right people, information, tools, assets to perform role
■ Flow of ideas, practices and expertise across business units		■ Empowerment and passion to lead, influence, change

- To add more rigour to the management reporting of KM projects;
- To provide KM project managers with quantifiable targets.

Effective scorecard metrics relate to outcomes rather than activities or milestones, so the starting point is a rigorous creation of KM outcomes. The next step is to define how to measure individual projects. Finally, the projects are linked via the overall KM outcomes. In this way the scorecard is used to link a macro and micro approach to measuring KM. As Figure 2 illustrates, the outcomes relate to the internal business environment, including systems and processes, and the behaviours of those working within it.

Project Scorecards

As every KM project has a business sponsor, a project scorecard is used to identify the operational outcomes. These scorecards are divided into three sections: purpose, objectives and goals.

- **Purpose** – A single statement. KM projects usually seek to address a business issue by using a KM intervention, or to improve the operation of an existing KM intervention.
- **Objectives** – Each project should have one or more objectives. An objective is usually a high-level statement describing the impact of the project, rather than the deliverables or milestones. These explain what the project proposes to achieve and what is important to its success.

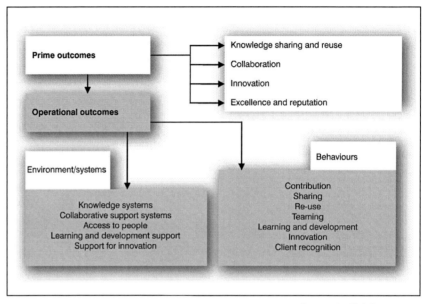

Figure 2: KM Outcomes

Objectives can be:
- KM-oriented;
- Business-oriented.

- **Goals** – The goals of a project specify what is to be measured in order to determine its success. Each goal consists of:
  - Measure: what is to be measured;
  - Target: the value to be achieved;
  - Date: the date by which that value is to be achieved. By repeating the same goal, but with different targets and dates, it is possible to plan for phased progress towards an objective;
- **Metric/method** – How the measurement will take place.

Each goal supports one or more objective.

Example project: Engagement Knowledgebase (EKB)

One example of a KM project is the Engagement Knowledgebase (EKB), an online tool available on Knowledge.net

Measuring the Value of Knowledge Management — Chapter 18

Goals (Measures)				Objectives
Engagement Knowledgebase (EKB)				
Purpose: Increase leverage of information, learnings and expertise from past engagements to more effectively sell and deliver new engagements	1. To encourage knowledge sharing through nominations or contributions	2. To increase general use of the EKB portal	3. To meet employees' needs for educational and reusable engagement-relevant knowledge	
No of engagements with assets in the EKB	Coverage		Coverage	
No of business units with engagement assets in the EKB	Coverage		Coverage	
Coverage in theatres per business unit launched	Coverage		Coverage	
Average asset educational value rating			Quality	
% of uses of EKB that results in one or more assets being reused		Quality	Quality	
Average user rating of satisfaction with the EKB			Quality	
No of unique users		Coverage		

☐ Operational outcomes   ▨ Prime outcomes

Figure 3: Project Scorecard for the EKB

Goal				
KM OUTCOME	Measure	Target	Timeframe	Metric/Notes on how measurement will be conducted
Engagement Knowledge Base (EKB)				
Purpose: Increase leverage of information, learnings and expertise from past engagements to more effectively sell and deliver new engagements				
Contribution	No of engagements with assets in EKB	300+	EO 2006	Count
	No of business units with engagement assets in the EKB	All	EO 2006	EKB Count. The business units are GFS, GOIS, GCI, GPS, S&T
	Coverage in theatres per business unit launched	NA/LA/UK	EO 2006	
Knowledge Systems	Average asset educational value rating	3.5 (out of 5)	EO 2006	Count
	% of uses of EKB that results in one or more assets being reused	10%	EO 2006	Ask survey question on extent to which user has re-used asst ('Use of EKB' means one user accessing it once)
	Average user rating of satisfaction with the EKB	4 out of 5	EO 2006	Survey
Re-Use	Total no of unique users		EO 2006	WebTrends report

☐ Operational outcomes   ▨ Prime outcomes

Figure 4: Defining the metrics

that was developed with the purpose of leveraging company experience to win new business. It enables employees throughout the organisation to:

- Find engagements by client solution, geography, value, business unit and asset type;
- View engagements in brief and drill down for details and key assets;
- Download engagement summaries for offline viewing and searching.

Measuring the Value of Knowledge Management   Chapter 18

Figure 3 is a summary of its project scorecard. The goals were then defined in detail and measured against the outcomes as depicted in Figure 4 below.

The final step in the process is to provide an aggregate measure for each project against relevant outcomes and to aggregate individual project scores across each outcome for a programme score.

KM outcomes

Key to the effectiveness of the KM scorecard are the KM outcomes against which the scores are measured. These need to fulfil several specific criteria. They should be usable as a way of structuring the KM scorecard; it should be possible to relate the goals of the KM projects to them; and they should be orthogonal – i.e. no outcome should depend on another outcome. Most importantly, they should be real KM outcomes, not the tactics used to achieve them. In this way, the scorecard measures the value of KM against projected outcomes at every strategic level. The following paragraphs list the outcomes that underpin KM measurement at Unisys. Each outcome is followed by its defining statement and an outline of the tools and processes it relates to.

Unisys defines its Prime KM outcomes – the highest level of KM outcomes – as follows.

- **Sharing and Re-use**: Our employees and business partners employ relevant and timely knowledge and skills to optimise process execution.
- **Collaboration**: Projects and programmes are resourced by collaborative teams that enhance the value created by the knowledge and skills of the individual members.
- **Innovation**: Opportunities are exploited to create new business value for Unisys from the knowledge and insight of our employees and business partners.
- **Excellence and Reputation**: Unisys has a world-class ability to manage and apply knowledge and expertise for the improvement of business performance. This is recognised by our key clients.

Operational KM outcomes are more specific. The following outcomes relate to business systems and environment.

- **Knowledge Systems:** Our employees and business partners have convenient access to knowledge systems that provide relevant and timely knowledge:
  – To help them optimise process execution;
  – To support collaborative teams.
  This outcome covers more of our activities than any other. It is concerned with:
  – The existence of knowledge repositories of any form;
  – The ease of access to them;
  – The quality and relevance of the information within them.

- **Collaborative Support Systems**: Our employees and partners have convenient access to collaboration support systems that help them maximise team effectiveness. This outcome is concerned with:
  – The existence of technology and support of collaborative tools such as Team Sites, Messenger, Live Meeting, Wikis, etc;
  – The ease of access to them.

- **Access to People**: Our employees and partners have convenient access to people with relevant skills and expertise:
  – To help them optimise process execution;

- To help them form collaborative teams;
- To help them exploit new business value.

This outcome is concerned with any systems or processes that make it easier to find people with specific skills or expertise.

- **Learning and Development Support:** Our employees have convenient access to relevant and timely learning and development opportunities:
  - To help them optimise process execution.

  This outcome is concerned with courses and formal learning rather than KM learning.

- **Support for Innovation:** Systems and processes are in place to rapidly exploit ideas for new business value. This outcome is concerned with any organisational systems that support the creation of new ideas and their conversion into business value.

  Other key outcomes relate to the behaviour of employees and other stakeholders. These are critical success factors for the company's KM programme.

- **Contribution:** Our employees and partners participate in the population of relevant knowledge systems.

  This outcome relates to person-to-system sharing, i.e. that people help to populate the EKB and post their learnings to a lessons learned database, etc.

- **Sharing:** Our employees and business partners share their knowledge and expertise with anyone in Unisys to whom it may be useful.

This outcome is concerned with people to people sharing, such as:
- Responding to telephone calls for help from outside your business unit;
- Offering to be a mentor;
- Presenting at community seminar sessions;
- Adding your name to a peer advisor list.

- **Re-use:** Our employees and business partners make appropriate re-use of existing artefacts, knowledge and skills:
  - To provide optimum outcomes;
  - To avoid re-creating work already done;
  - To avoid repeating past mistakes.

  This outcome is concerned with consciously searching for things such as reusable artefacts and lessons that others have learned.

- **Teaming:** Our employees and business partners create and work together as high-performing teams, ensuring they are properly resourced and operate based on common understandings and values.

  This outcome is concerned with good teaming and collaborative behaviours.

- **Learning and development:** Our employees use learning and development opportunities to keep their knowledge and skills up to date.

  This outcome is concerned with behaviours such as creating and following a learning path.

- **Innovation:** Our employees and business partners create ideas for new business value from their knowledge and insights.

  This outcome is concerned with the behaviour of innovation and creating new business value.

- **Client recognition**: Unisys is recognised by our key clients for its world-class ability to manage and apply knowledge and expertise for the improvement of business performance.

    This outcome is concerned with our clients' behaviour: we wish them to recognise our world-class abilities. However, to achieve such recognition would require achieving recognition within the industry, which represents a tactic rather than an outcome.

Separating outcomes from tactics

Finally, it is crucial to differentiate outcomes from tactics, and this is not always straightforward. For example, if the following tactics were used as outcomes, the KM scorecard could well produce a very different set of metrics.

- **Learning about KM** – this is an achieving tactic to support other outcomes such as the use of collaborative and other KM tools.
- **Reward and recognition** – this is a tactic to encourage the behaviours identified as outcomes.
- **Regulatory compliance** – this is a requirement rather than an outcome.

Alex Goodall is principle KM consultant, Global KM Programme, Unisys Ltd. He can be contacted at alex.goodall@gb.unisys.com

Index

A
ABN AMRO Bank, 39
Admired Knowledge Enterprise, 2-3, 57
AIDS, 90
American Productivity, 2, 7, 20-21, 27, 70
AOL, 17, 31
Aon, 7
APQC, 2, 20, 70
APQC KM Measurement Bell Curve, 20
ARC, 19, 46-47
Aristotle, 81
Ark, 1-2, 4, 7, 12, 20-21, 27-28, 49, 107
Ash, Jerry, 12, 21, 27
Assets Monitor, 18
Automotive Industries, 65

B
BAE SYSTEMS, 2, 7, 12, 41, 43
Bair, Jim, 1, 9
Balanced Scorecard, 2, 15-16, 18, 33, 46, 48-49, 71, 83, 107
Bater, Bob, 7, 20-21
Belgium, 79
Benefits, 1-3, 5-6, 11-14, 16-17, 20, 25-27, 43, 45-46, 48, 54-55, 58-59, 66, 70-71, 81-83, 89-90
Benefits Tree, 2, 16-17
Berwin Leighton Paisner, 2, 4, 19, 45-46, 49
Best Practice, 2-3, 5-6, 12, 41-43, 64, 67
Black Belt, 64, 66
BP, 23, 26, 73
BPR, 64, 66
Britain, 85
British Standards Institute, 47, 49
BT, 77
Budget, 41, 70, 74
Business-based KPIs, 5-6

C
Canada, 63
CapGemini, 23
CARE International UK, 90
Caterpillar Inc, 2

Caterpillar University, 51, 55
Champions, 72, 79, 81-82
Chevron Texaco, 23
China, 98
Collison, Chris, 87, 89
COI, 13
Collaboration, 4-6, 14, 38, 41, 43, 51-52, 54-55, 58, 69, 71-74, 80, 83, 85, 88, 90, 107, 111
Commercialisation, 47
Communicate, 16, 24, 26-27, 37-38, 60, 82, 99
Communication, 37, 54, 79-80, 82, 85, 90, 102, 104
Community, 25, 52-55, 57, 60-61, 63-64, 66, 70-73, 77-83, 93, 102, 104, 112
Competence, 18, 38
Competencies Framework, 87-90
Compliance, 9
Consulting, 12, 25, 28, 47, 73, 100, 107
COO, 74-75
CoPs, 6, 12, 16, 20, 25, 27, 53, 93
Costs, 1-4, 6-7, 9-13, 15, 23, 27, 35, 42, 59-60, 64-67, 71, 78
Courtney Consulting, 47
Coverage, 109-110
Credit, 64-66
CSOs, 90
Culture, 3, 6, 27, 58, 60-61, 78-81, 99, 107
Customer Satisfaction, 1, 5, 7, 15, 25, 47, 54, 63-66, 78
Customer Solutions, 42
Czech Republic, 79

D

Dell, 15, 21, 70, 74
Delphi Group, 24, 37
Desktop Re-life, 42
Development Portfolio, 42
Discussion, 16, 26, 34-35, 54, 57, 70, 93
Dow Chemical, 23

E

Ecuador, 90
Effective KM, 1-3, 9, 17-18, 23, 58-59, 83
Egypt, 72
Ei, 1-2
Electronic, 24, 54, 72-73, 93, 104
Energy, 27, 29, 66, 69, 73
Engagement, 25, 108-110
Engineering, 10, 42, 57, 60-61, 95, 98, 100, 103-105

ENR, 57
Entrepreneurship, 39
Europe, 41, 77-79, 81
Evaluating KM, 3, 25, 93
Excel, 15, 42, 64, 105
ExxonMobil, 73

F
Feedback, 2, 11, 16, 25, 47, 49, 52, 59, 82
Financial, 5, 9, 13-19, 25, 33, 45, 48, 71, 74, 83, 90, 96, 102, 107
Five Competencies Framework, 87-90
Fluor Corporation, 2, 57, 61
Ford Explorer, 63
Ford Financial-Global, 64
Ford Motor Company, 2, 63-65, 67
Framework, 13-14, 19-20, 29, 31, 33-35, 78-79, 81, 85, 87-90
Frappaolo, Carl, 2, 9

G
Gartner, 34
Gatekeeper, 65-66
Gatewest, 41
GE Plastics, 23
Germany, 79, 98
Global Experts, 60
Global KM Programme, 113
Global Knowledge, 3, 11, 61
Goodall, Alex, 113
Group-status, 102
Gurteen, David, 31

H
Halliburton KM, 69, 71-75
Harvard, 48
Health Service KM, 85
Hewlett Packard, 10, 25
High Value Outcomes, 30
HIV, 90
Holistic View of Knowledge, 86
Holy Grail, 33, 59
Houston, 70, 72
HP Services Consulting, 12, 28
HR, 41, 46, 59, 74, 79, 103
HVo, 30

I
IBM Global Services, 23
ICT, 36-38, 98
IFIs, 90
Incentives, 7, 88
India, 98
Information Services, 98, 105
Innovation, 2, 4, 6, 9, 11, 15-19, 31, 38-39, 43, 47-48, 53, 59, 70, 74, 78, 97, 107, 112
Inside Knowledge, 1-2, 7, 27-28, 75, 95
Intangible Assets, 2-3, 10, 12, 17-19, 24, 45-46, 48, 101
Integration, 12, 28, 42, 58, 74, 80, 82, 107
Intellectual Capital, 1-3, 10-13, 16-19, 45, 47, 51, 57
Intelligent Learning Portal, 42
International Development, 85, 90-91, 93-94
Internet, 17, 51-52, 58-59, 73, 77, 98, 101, 105
Intranet, 27, 42, 46, 58, 93, 101
IP, 10, 90, 102
Iske, Paul, 2, 39
Italy, 79, 98

J
Japan, 98
Japanese, 102

K
Kaplan, Robert, 48
KBR, 69, 73-75
KITs, 45
KM Outcomes, 12, 15, 20, 108, 111, 113
KM Scorecard, 107, 111, 113
KM Vision, 107
Knowledge Activist, 31
Knowledge Audit, 24, 26-27, 87
Knowledge Capture, 85, 88, 90
Knowledge Creating Company, 81
Knowledge Network, 51-52
Knowledge OnLine, 58-59, 61
Knowledgebase, 77-78, 81-82, 104, 108-109
Korea, 98
KPIs, 5-6, 46-47

L
Laboratory, 101
Labour, 1, 4-6

Launch KM, 20
Law Library Resource Xchange, 21
Leadership, 1, 10, 23, 38, 65, 67, 74, 80
Learning Specialist, 85, 91, 94
Learning Tools Measuring, 86
Legal, 6-7, 13, 20-21, 45-47, 52, 82, 96, 99, 102
Leif Edvinsson, 1, 17
Leverage, 9, 14, 37, 42, 51, 55, 57-59, 63-65, 69, 77, 107, 109-110
Library, 21, 24, 41, 93, 101-102, 104-105
Lucent Technologies, 2, 77, 83

M

MAKE, 1-3, 7, 13-14, 17, 29-30, 35, 39, 46-49, 57-60, 65, 69, 95, 105, 112
Making Knowledge Work, 3-4, 7, 9, 12, 26, 28
Management Systems, 12, 74-75
Manufacturing, 41-42, 63, 74, 100
Mapping, 2, 24, 89
Marconi, 77
Marketing, 29, 46, 52, 74, 99, 102
Media, 41, 102, 107
Medical, 66
Meta-knowledge, 104
Methodologies, 1-2, 5, 12-13, 20, 28, 33, 46, 70
Metrics, 1-3, 5-7, 9-12, 17, 20, 23-27, 45-49, 63, 65-67, 79-81, 101-105, 108, 113
Microsoft, 17, 42
Motivation, 37, 66
Motorola, 26

N

NASDAQ, 3
Navigation, 19
Navy KM Measurement Categories Usage, 2, 19
NeLH, 24, 27
Netherlands, 34, 39, 79
Network Analysis, 87
Networks, 6, 37, 41, 54, 77, 81, 88, 90
New Delhi, 57
Newman, Victor, 2, 31
New York, 21
Next Generation Knowledge, 9, 12, 17, 21, 27
NGOs, 85-86
Nigel Courtney, 47, 49
Nonaka, 81
Norton, David, 2, 15, 48

O
Operational KM, 111
Outcomes, 1-2, 4, 6, 10, 12, 15-16, 18-20, 23, 25, 30, 78, 95, 105, 108-113
Outlook, 42
Outputs, 12, 14, 23, 45, 47, 93
Overseas, 2, 57-58, 85, 91, 94
Overseas Development Institute, 2, 85, 91, 94

P
PAR, 78-79
Parcell, Geoff, 87, 89
Partnership Programme, 90
Patents, 102
PC, 73, 77
Peer Assists, 93
People Value, 41
PeopleFinder, 34, 36-38
Periodicals, 102, 105
PhDs, 70, 103-104
Poland, 79
Policy, 65, 85-87, 91, 94
Portals, 12, 37
Portugal, 79
PPP, 90
Process-based KPIs, 5-6
Procurement, 10, 42, 57, 71-72, 74
Project Scorecard, 108-109, 111

Q
Quality Assurance, 59
Quality Center, 2, 7, 20-21, 27, 70
Quality Leadership Initiative, 65
Quality research, 65
Quantitative, 2, 12, 14-15, 19-20, 25, 33, 36, 39, 47, 101

R
Reciprocity, 74
Reinvestment, 1, 4
Resource Centre, 42
Ricardo Consulting Engineers, 100
Ricardo Knowledge Community, 104
Ricardo Knowledgebase, 104
Ricardo16, 95
ROI of KM, 3, 20, 23, 25

Rolls-Royce, 27-28
Russia, 79

S
SAP, 71-73
SAS, 30
Saudi Arabia, 72
SECI, 81
Services Department, 98, 105
Shell, 23, 61, 73
6 Sigma, 65, 71
Significant Change, 87
SiteScape, 61
Skandia, 18, 33
Skyrme Associates, 2, 12, 16-17, 21, 28
Skyrme, David, 10, 11, 16, 27
SNA, 87
Snowden, David, 81
South Africa, 57
Spain, 79
Squarewise, 39
Standard KM, 37
Standards, 33, 47, 49, 54, 65, 74
STAR Series Dialogue, 75
Steve Denning, 27, 81
Storage, 85, 88, 90, 93
Strategic Consulting, 100
Strategy Development, 85, 87-89
Supercomputing Applications, 51
Superknowledge Declaration, 29-30
Supply Chain, 74-75
Sveiby, Karl-Erik, 1, 8, 11, 12, 17-18, 21, 33
System-user, 49
Systems Community, 61

T
Tacit, 13, 38, 81, 104-105
Technical Specialists, 104
Technical Support Service, 98
Technicians, 72-73, 103-104
Technologies, 2, 37, 59, 77, 83, 97
Teleos, 3, 7
Time-based KPIs, 5
Training, 6-7, 12-13, 30, 41-42, 46, 49, 52-53, 55, 59, 72-73, 78, 80, 86, 90, 100

U
UK, 27, 42, 79-80, 82-83, 85, 90-91, 94, 98
Unique Chat Hosts, 93
Unisys, 107, 111-113
University, 12, 31, 41, 43, 51, 55
US Army, 26

V
Valuation of Knowledge Potential, 35
Value Methodology, 19
Value Wheel, 1, 4
Value-chain, 51-52
Virtual University, 12, 41

W
WIFM, 6
Wikis, 111
Windows XP, 42
World Bank, 23